W9-BJG-670

Letters *from* PRAGUE
1939-1941

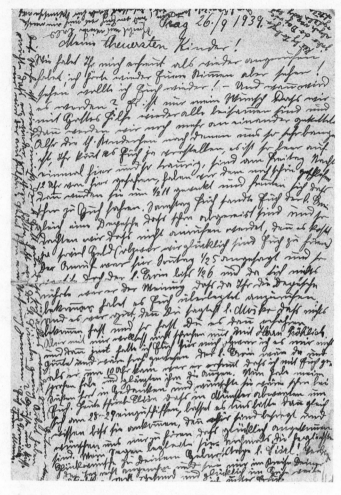

OBVERSE OF A POSTCARD FROM PAULA
DATED SEPTEMBER 26, 1939 (LETTER 23)

Letters
from
PRAGUE
1939-1941

COMPILED BY
RAYA CZERNER SCHAPIRO
HELGA CZERNER WEINBERG

Academy Chicago Publishers

Paperback edition published in 1996 by
Academy Chicago Publishers
363 West Erie Street
Chicago, Illinois 60610

© 1991 Raya Czerner Schapiro and Helga CzernerWeinberg

"She Remembers 'Eleanor'" by Gladys Damon,
is reprinted by permission of *The Jewish Advocate*,
Boston, Mass.

Printed and bound in the U.S.A.

No part of this book may be reproduced in any form
without the express written permission of the publisher.

Library of Congress Cataloging-in-Publication Data

Letters from Prague, 1939–1941 / compiled by Raya Czerner
    Schapiro, Helga Czerner Weinberg.
        p.   cm.
    Includes bibliographical references and index.
    ISBN 0-89733-369-1 (hardcover)
    ISBN 0-89733-427-2 (paperback)
    1. Jews—Czechoslovakia—Prague—Coorespondence.
2. Holocaust, Jewish (1939–1945)—Czechoslovakia—
Prague—Sources. 3. Prague (Czechoslovakia)—Ethnic
relations. I. Schapiro, Raya Czerner, 1934–   . II. Weinberg,
Helga Czerner, 1932–
DS135.C96P7454   1991
940.53'18'0922—dc20
[B]
                                            91-30999
                                              CIP

DEDICATED TO THE MEMORY OF
PAULA FROEHLICH (1876–1942)
AND ERWIN FROEHLICH (1903–1943)

Although they went to their deaths as No. 796 and No. 539, it is our hope that publishing their words will restore the precious names of our beloved Grandmother Paula and her son, our adored Uncle Erwin.

Our Thanks:

To our wonderful friend, Dr Ruth Pick (who knew Erwin when she was a medical student in Prague), who spent countless hours translating our grandmother's spidery Gothic German script and her crowded, colloquial Czech sentences — which became less and less legible with time, as paper supplies decreased and anxiety increased. In addition to her linguistic expertise, Ruth lent valuable insight to the censored content of the letters since she too was in Prague during the years they were written.

To our mother's dear cousin, Dr Edith Vogl-Garrett,who provided a wealth of information about many of our relatives and their fates.

To Ivan Bernasek, a friend who found the letters amid piles of junk while helping to clear out our parents' apartment, and who also helped with some of the Czech translation.

To Drs Helmut Baum and Michael Franz Basch for some additional help in translating from the German.

To a great friend, Michael Boroian, who unstintingly, enthusiastically and generously provided hours and hours of typing help — which may have cost him his job!

To Professor Peter Hayes, whose historical expertise helped all those involved.

To Dr Leopold Rozboril and Mrs Olga Kovar, of the Czech National Council (Chicago), and to Dr Frank Svejkovsay, for their friendly assistance during the fact-checking stages.

Our gratitude to Dr Anita Miller, Michele Tucker, Sarah Leslie Welsch and Julia Anderson Miller of Academy Chicago Publishers, who worked with extraordinary dedication to help us turn a collection of letters into a readable book. A special thanks is due Sarah Welsch, whose scholarly research for the historical annotations to the letters added an important dimension to this personal account.

And to our mother, for preserving this rich legacy.

CONTENTS

Photographs follow page 100

Editors' Note

These letters were written originally in German and Czech: letters to and from the children in Czech; letters to and from the adults in German. The letters have been edited to some extent: they have been broken into paragraphs for easier reading, although it should be remembered that paper was scarce in Prague and the Froehlichs filled every inch of the letters with writing — even the margins. Editorial emendations appear enclosed in brackets.

Each letter is numbered. However, often several letters were sent together: when this is clear, we counted this group of letters as one. Often, too, additions were made to the letters over a period of days, so within one group of letters, dates may vary. An occasional letter is undated: in these cases, we used internal evidence to place them, and enclosed the putative date in brackets.

Irma's letters are extant in the form of rough drafts which she made and kept. Max made carbon copies of his letters. Paula's last postcard was sent to Irma after the war by her cousin Aninka Brezak.

When appropriate, notes follow the letters. There are two types of notes: they are differentiated by the way in which they are printed. Notes of explanation and amplification are set in Roman type, although the first time an individual is mentioned in the notes, the name alone is italicized. Notes on laws or official restrictions and the progress of the war are printed in italic type throughout. When possible, the laws are described following letters to which they seem appropriate; if there are no appropriate comments in the letters, the laws are inserted following letters with an appropriate date. Each law has a bracketed date which refers to the time when the law was codified, ratified or otherwise officially proclaimed. It should be noted that laws and proclamations were frequently put into effect long before their official appearance on the books.

Members of the Froehlich and Czerner families are identified in the notes, and also in the index. Further aid is provided by the family trees. Non-family members are also identified in the notes and in the index. Names of people who cannot be identified have been included in the index so that anyone who might be able to identify them can do so.

On March 15, 1939, we stood at the window and watched German tanks roll into our city. Our mother, holding our five-month-old brother, stood with us as we waited for our father to make his way home from his office through the clogged streets. The fact that the German military headquarters was established directly opposite our apartment building made it seem as if the entire invading army was converging on us personally. Within the hour, hordes of goose-stepping "green men" poured into the square, and we saw for the first time the gigantic swastika banner unfurled from the balcony across the street.

The way of life that ended for us that day had been gracious and comfortable. We lived in a spacious apartment in the most modern building in Prague with our parents (Irma and Max), our brand-new baby brother (Tomichek), a nursemaid, a cook, a housekeeper and a chauffeur. German and Czech were spoken in our home about equally and we were fluent in both, although German was used more by adults speaking to one another, and Czech reserved mainly for children, servants and the street.

Our maternal grandmother Paula, widowed in 1936, lived nearby and visited with us and our mother daily. We saw our beloved uncle Erwin — our mother's only sibling — a bit less often, since he was a busy and dedicated physician and a bachelor with an active social life, but he was definitely part of our close family circle.

Our father's relatives, by contrast, were almost strangers to us: they lived far across town and visited us rarely; they spoke primarily Yiddish and Russian, which we did not understand. We hardly knew our paternal grand-mother, Bathsheva, or our father's brother Elisha with whom we eventually made the trip to America.

Immediately after the Occupation, the frantic struggle for visas, exit permits and affidavits began. Although we were five and seven years old at the time, the tense late-night discussions we overheard, and the frightened faces of the heretofore serene adults in our lives, told us much.

It was feared that prominent Jews were in special danger, and that our father's position as General Director of Shell Oil Company put him on the Nazi list for imminent arrest. (This fear was far from groundless; it was learned later that Leo Schwab, a Jew and Director of Shell Oil for Lithuania, was shot in the company offices immediately following the Nazi occupation of that country.) Therefore, at the risk of death if he were betrayed or discovered, our father entered into clandestine negotiations with a German officer who wanted our luxurious apartment for his secret Czech mistress. Exit visas would be provided for our family, and the vacated apartment would be discreetly confiscated.

At the very last moment, however, the German officer produced only three of the five exit permits we needed. One can imagine the anxiety and distress of our parents at this juncture: our father almost certainly on a Nazi death-list; our mother still nursing an infant; two small girls — and only three visas! After many assurances from their friend the American Consul (who lived in our building) that we would be given two more exit visas in a matter of days, our parents made the painful decision to flee with our infant brother while they could.

Thus, in May of 1939, we were left with Paula and Erwin who had always been part of our daily lives and with whom we felt completely at home. We lived under their anxious, protective care in ever-smaller quarters through the first shocking months of the Occupation.

Entry into the United States was possible for our Russian-born father and his immediate family because the Russian quota was wide open; the Czech quota, however, was extremely small and entry was almost impossible for our Czech-born maternal relatives. It turned out that our parents' departure deprived us of the benefit of the Russian quota. Therefore, although exit visas were available for us, months passed as various emigration plans were considered for us: to travel to relative safety in England with a boatload of children (the "Rubesova project" mentioned in the letters) or alone to England or Holland or Trieste, where our father would meet us and take us to America under the Russian quota — many, many plans over many months.

Finally, our father succeeded in arranging for us to travel in the care of his Russian-born brother Elisha and his family. On the eve of Yom Kippur, September 22, 1939, a taxi with blue headlights drove us through the blacked-out streets of Prague to the railway station. There we said a tearful goodbye to our grandmother and uncle. From the feeling of sadness we recall to this day, it is certain that not one of the four of us believed the empty phrases we were repeating about seeing each other again soon.

We remember in fragments the train trip through

Germany to Holland: Elisha's nervousness and fits of temper; long stops, with uniformed men boarding the train to check papers; sleeping and waking over and over again. We made it to Holland only to be turned back to Germany because the boat on which we had booked passage had already left, and we had no "papers" allowing us to stay in Holland to await the next ship. (In fact, the ship that sailed without us hit a mine in the Atlantic, with great loss of life. When our parents heard news reports in the U.S. of this catastrophe, they had not yet learned that we had missed that ship.) Helga recalls that, with incredible resourcefulness and fast-talking, Elisha persuaded the Dutch authorities to let us at least stay the night in Holland after our exhausting trip. Then, through a network of volunteers that provided food and shelter for Jews in transit, Elisha found places for us to stay in Germany. We remember splitting up and staying in crowded houses with other refugees, going out only once a day after dark to eat soup at long tables with strangers.

After several such weeks we returned to Holland to board the *Rotterdam*, which sailed from the port of the same name. We will always remember being awakened on the drizzly grey morning of October 29, 1939, and hustled sleepily up on deck to see the Statue of Liberty as we sailed into New York Harbor. Our father's was one of the many, many hands joyously waving on the dock.

Between June 1939 and September 1941, our grandmother Paula Froehlich wrote these loving, yearning letters to her daughter, Irma (nicknamed "Imschko" and "Shishinko") and her son-in-law Max ("Moshko"), often referring to us by our pet names "Helgichka" and Rayushka". Our uncle Erwin also wrote to them, and to us. The letters were saved by our mother and found in one heartbreaking collection after our father's death in 1988. Each has a censor's number pencilled on it, and each envelope bears the still-frightening emblem of the Third Reich.

Some of the letters were written by Erwin to his friend in New York, Dr Joseph Sperling (now retired and living in Philadelphia). A few rough drafts from Irma and carbon-copies from Max of letters to Prague were found and included. There are even some childishly-scrawled letters from us to our parents in the early months of our separation. The last postcard, written by Paula to her sister in another Czech town on July 1, 1942 was sent to us after the war by Irma's surviving cousin, Aninka.

As the Appendix shows, Paula was deported from Prague to the concentration camp of Theresienstadt on July 9, 1942, and from there to the extermination camp of Treblinka on October 19, 1942. To the best of our knowledge she was gassed on her 66th birthday, October 23, 1942. Erwin was sent to Theresienstadt on November 20, 1942, and to his immediate death in the gas-chamber of Auschwitz on January 21, 1943, at age 39. We learned this horrendous news in bits and pieces over the post-war years, and may never know the dates and places of the murders of Max's mother and sisters.

When we read these letters, we hear again the beloved voices of our grandmother and uncle, and feel again our brief but powerful attachment to them. Since countless others died in those times and left no trace, we are grateful that the words of Paula and Erwin are preserved in these pages, an indelible record that will outlive our memories.

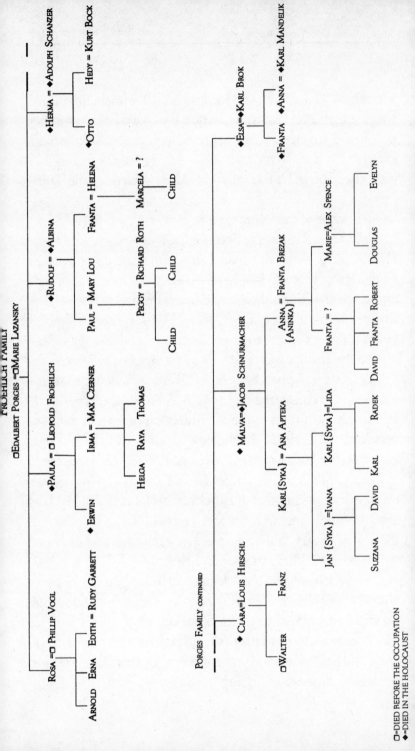

FROEHLICH FAMILY
□Edalbert Porges =□Marie Lazansky

□=DIED BEFORE THE OCCUPATION
◆=DIED IN THE HOLOCAUST

Porges Family continued

CZERNER FAMILY

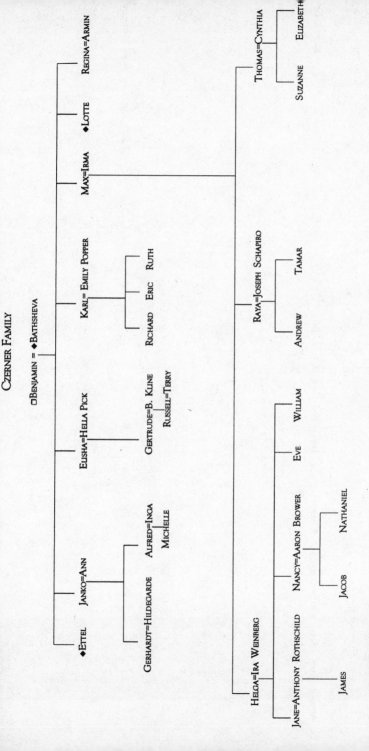

□=DIED BEFORE THE OCCUPATION
◆=DIED IN THE HOLOCAUST

THE LETTERS

In mid-March, 1939 Germany occupied Czechoslovakia, then to be known as the Reich Protectorate of Bohemia and Moravia, under Reich Protector Baron Constantin von Neurath.

The following month the first anti-Semitic legislation was enacted defining "Jewishness" and restricting the number of Jews who could practice certain professions.

Letter 1   Prikope 35
From Paula   Prague
                                                           June 21, 1939

MY DEAREST CHILDREN,

We were very happy to get your letters — I'm so glad that you seized the opportunity and left. God will help you, and I pray for you, my children. My thoughts are with you, even when I don't write. I don't have much time, I'm busy all day, and I have to get up early in the morning to write you — in the evening I'm too tired, and the dear little ones call me all the time and I have to tell them stories 'til they fall asleep. Both of them fight over me, so I have to go from one to the other and tell something to each one; so I have to think up all kinds of things. In the morning I take them with me shopping, and then we go out again. After eating I put them down for a nap and in the afternoon we go out again. Both of them look very well, knock on wood, and also dear Rayushka has her happy face back again. They are both very good, especially Helgichka, and she is very understanding. Dear Rayushka can be very charming even when she is angry — so it's necessary to have strong nerves. But she is still little, and she'll grow up to be good. Both are very clever, and I'm going to miss them a lot.

They also have a good time with Erwin, and he amuses them — it's a pleasure to see it. They are both happy when their uncle takes time to be with them and play with them and tell them stories — for which, unfortunately, there is enough time because he does not have many patients. Yesterday was a nice day and there was no rain. I haven't had time to look for someone to help with the children because I am busy with them all day; and it doesn't pay for only a few weeks. I'll stick it out. How do I know when they will go? I would like it best if Armin could take them along. He said that perhaps he won't be going. We have taken the apartment on Masna Street, opposite the place where dear Shishinko went to school, and I showed the little ones the school.

The rent [of the new apartment] is 14,500 Kr. including heat and water, and there is a concierge. But, if my wishes could be granted. . . .

I worry very much about you. Dear Mother Czerner no longer worries. I wanted to visit her but Elisha doesn't want me to go. And Erwin cannot go because of Lotte. So we'll have to wait until Mother comes to us. She would get so much pleasure out of seeing the girls — they don't even know her. But Elisha doesn't want it, so we have to go along with his wishes. When you called at eleven o'clock, Erwin had already left and he came home late and didn't know, Moshko, that you were going to call and he was very sorry he couldn't talk to you so I had to talk and I wrote everything down and in the morning I went to Armin immediately and to Elisha. I was happy that the children heard your voices, even briefly. If only Erwin were already taken care of. But — you understand me. I yearn for you and I still thank God and hope everything turns out well. From my last letter, you know we had to give up the big apartment and sell everything in it for 350 Kr.! And I was happy to find buyers! If I hadn't, "they" would have taken everything away. Tonscha [a maid] and the nursemaid were also fine ones! But let's not talk about that, it doesn't pay to get upset about it. What's gone is gone — we just want peace. You asked about our sleeping arrangements — Mr Rosenthal would have liked to stay with us, but I told him that I need the room for the children — so he wasn't happy about it but he left and the children sleep in beds for a change and are very proud that they have their own room. Rosenthal comes daily to see us and would like to live with us again. I will see — I would like to have a boarder.

Now, to continue: today I sent Zanka [a housekeeper] out with the children so I could rest a little. Since today is Wednesday you are probably already in your new situation — God be with you and give you health and happiness. Write us when you have time, about the trip and how Tomichek is; whether you have a good apartment, and what your impressions are, and about everything because I am curious about everything. Before, I could just run to you and check out everything — now that's not possible. Aunt Rosa already packed everything but she can't send it yet, it was stopped. Arnold would have liked to speak to you, Moshko. Today we received a letter from Sperling. I hope you will get together and we'll hear more. We're now getting ready to move so I'll be busy again but then I won't have much time. Perhaps Aunt Elsa will help me. And I'll give the little ones to Elisha.

WE CONTINUE WELL — BIG KISSES FROM

YOUR MOTHER

✉

Armin Davidovic was married to Max's sister *Regina.*

Elisha was Max's brother (married to *Hella*)

Max, Elisha and Regina — and in fact all seven of the Czerner siblings — were born in Russia; they were therefore eligible for American visas, since the Russian immigration quota was not filled: Soviet Russia did not allow emigration. Erwin and Paula, on the other hand, had been born in Czechoslovakia and the Czech U. S. quota was filled. There was a long waiting list.

The children had to be accompanied to America by an adult. Paula preferred that Armin accompany them rather than Elisha, who had a difficult personality.

Mother Czerner (Bathsheva), Max's mother, lived in the Bulharska section of Prague with two unmarried daughters: Ettel and Lotte — who was lame and in poor health. Although all three women qualified for the Russian quota, Lotte's health apparently put her admission to the U.S. in question. Mother Czerner refused to leave Lotte and did not want to emigrate in any case, although her eldest son Janko already lived in New York.

It is not clear why Elisha did not want Paula to visit Mother Czerner. It is certainly known that there was bad feeling between the Czerners and Erwin because heavy pressure had been put on Erwin to marry Lotte and he had stead-fastly refused.

Paula and Erwin were being forced to move into the Masna Street apartment and to take in a boarder, probably primarily for financial reasons arising from the new Nazi laws.

Kr. is an abbreviation for the Czech crown. In 1939 there were approximately twenty-five crowns to the US dollar.

Aunt Rosa Vogl was Paula's sister; *Arnold* was Rosa's son, who had emigrated to America in 1938, but was in Prague visiting at this time.

Dr [Joseph] Sperling was a friend and former medical student of Erwin's who was able to emigrate. He wrote many letters on Erwin's behalf.

Elsa Brok was another of Paula's six siblings.

On June 21, 1939, the date of Paula's letter, Von Neurath issued a comprehensive decree which implemented the Nuremberg racial laws of 1935 and excluded Jews from economic activity: they could not sell or transfer real estate, businesses or securities without permission. They had to report the possession of all precious metals, pearls and art objects by July 31, 1939.

✉

Letter 2   Prikope 35
From Erwin   Prague
                                                        June, 1939

DEAR IRMA AND MOSHKO:

Now you have reached the goal of your long travel —I congratulate you. I wish you much luck in your undertaking — much success and contentment. I wanted our letter to get there before your arrival in New York, but the present difficulties and work etc. make it impossible to write often. Helgichka is my little "assistant" and while I'm writing this she moves around everywhere, dusts and cleans up. Raya of course does not want to be left out and she has appointed herself the assistant for the waiting room and wants to turn on the light for the patients which Zanka often does not do. If I'm not busy, they are buzzing around me constantly — even now as I write this. Yesterday Sharp came back. Today at eleven Elisha has an appointment with [illegible] and tomorrow I will go and see Sharp.

As for your mother [Czerner], the doctor did not want to remove the atheroma because it went too deep and he had no assistant, so it was taken care of at the Jewish clinic and fortunately is already healing.

Today I got a letter from Dr Sperling via *The Yankee Clipper* in which he recommends a doctor in Leeds, England, who would be willing to sponsor me and I would then be able to live there. I shall write him immediately. Also, he will get in touch with Froehlich from South Norwalk regarding affidavits for Mother and me. Then I got a letter from a London committee that my application would be put in the priority group of physicians who would be permitted to study and practice in

Great Britain. This will be decided in a few weeks.

We will move to Masna St., #19, first floor. It's a new building — three nice rooms, hallway, many built-in shelves, refrigerator in the kitchen. Because of the diathermy, etc. the rent is 14,500 Kr. It is also possible to rent out one room. It's very rainy here and the weather is bad. The Moldau is high and other rivers are flooding. Otherwise, there are many changes here since you left. All the other relatives are still here. Brok is even on summer vacation. And Tante Steffi is exactly as difficult as at the time you left — not better, as predicted.

Now, my assistants want to write so I will close with many kisses to all three of you and wish you luck in your new country. Now, I just got a call that I will have to pay your last telephone bill for 450 Kr., and since you don't want to have trouble with Mrs G. I shall pay the bill.

ERWIN

✉

Reverend *Sharp* was an American in charge of an emigration mission in Prague.

An atheroma is a benign fatty tumor.

"A doctor in Leeds" recommended by Dr Sperling was named Samuels. See *Letters* 3, 5 and 7. It was hoped that he would provide a guarantee for Erwin, but apparently he did not do so.

Affidavits were vouchers guaranteeing that the émigrés would not become financial burdens on the nations that accepted them. The signer of the affidavit testified to the wage-earning ability of the applicant and promised to take financial responsibility for him or her if that should become necessary. At this time, affidavits could be supplied only by a relative who was also an American citizen, but these rules kept changing.

Diathermy is heat therapy through electric current.

The Moldau River runs through Prague.

Brok was Aunt Elsa's husband, Karl.

The Froehlichs and the Czerners had agreed to refer to the Nazis by the code name *Tante Steffi.*

The identity of "Mrs G" is not clear. One guess is that this name refers to the Nazi official who took over Max and Irma's apartment — or to the Czech mistress whom he installed there. The phone bill must be one that Max owed when he fled Prague.

✉

Letter 3   Prikope 35
From Erwin to Dr Joseph Sperling   Prague
                                                June 27, 1939

DEAR JOSEPH,

Only yesterday, the 26th, I got your letter from June 11th — that is one week later then the one from the 16th, which was sent by *The Yankee Clipper*. I am very curious about what news I will get from Dr Samuels in Leeds. I am very thankful for this opportunity and for the generous invitation from Mr Green. Although it takes a long time to get the English permit and visa, it is still a good feeling to know that I might have another option besides the USA.

Through my brother-in-law, I met an American here who has an emigration mission, and this man (named Rev. Sharp) has taken my *curriculum vitae* along to London and Paris. The result, as he reported, is approximately as follows: "I was in London June 12–14; there, I presented your case in the Medical Committee. I have no news except to say that you are registered with them — along with 400 other Czech doctors." However, I got news that I was put in the group of doctors allowed to practice in England — but the final decision on this will be made in a few months. This is a small hope. According to Sharp, there are several options, and he thinks I should interest myself in the possibility of going to Chile: "Jewish people are welcome there but must have 1200 pesos in landing money." He gave me the address of a Miss Marie Ginsberg, *Comité pour le Placement des Intellectuels* in Geneva, Switzerland, with a recommendation, and I wrote to her last week. So another plan: Chile. He also told me: "Most South American countries want only professing

Roman Catholics. Most of the medical missions want only Evangelical Protestants." And what does the USA want?

This time you have told us something about yourself. I am happy that you opted for Connecticut to establish your practice because New York is overcrowded with doctors. Perhaps you will settle in Norwalk, which will be very good and you will also have your hospital nearby. As far as your future plans are concerned, you are making me very curious.

And now, there will soon be a Dr Jacob Greenbaum arriving in New York. He will be staying with Mr Herman N. Opper, New York City, 501 E. 161st Street. When you speak with him, please tell him I have not yet obtained the diploma — I inquired about it again yesterday. As soon as I get it, I will have it translated and notarized and will send it on.

In the next week or two I will write you only if I have something important to report because I will be very busy moving. My address is: Praha I, Masna Ulice 19.

I have not heard any news from my sister, who is now probably in N.Y. Aside from a telegram, it is unlikely that there would be any. She spoke to us on the phone from The Hague.

My nieces have gotten very used to me. Raya said to me today, "I don't want to go over the big ocean, because I would have to leave you here; but you could come right along, and we could share a practice, and I would wear a white coat with 'Assistant' written on it." Raya is five years old. It will not be so easy for the little ones to get a visa because if their father is not accompanying them they will not be considered under the Russian quota but under the Czech one.

Just now I received a cable from my sister: "Happy and healthy in N.Y."

Dr Schauer married an American woman three months ago. She was here for the purpose of a preferential visa; he is still here. This is a good example of your idea to marry!

What do you really intend to tell Frau Schanzer? It is regrettable that you have made so many frustrating attempts with regard to her. Just today I got an affidavit from the American consulate. I've had a photostat made in case I need it for the English permit. My average earnings amount to about 1000 Kr. per month. The consulate writes, with regard to my permit, "Under the present immigration laws it is assumed that your turn might be reached within approximately two years. This estimate of your waiting time is given without any obligation."

Cordial regards also from my mother and greetings to your parents and lots of luck on your examinations,

ERWIN

P.S. I wrote to Ing. Weinmann that you are sorry that you couldn't comply with his wishes and that the so-called *friendship affidavit* would not be recognized here. On my affidavit, Frau Schanzer describes me as "a distant relative of her late husband." I am very curious whether Mr Froehlich in South Norwalk will answer me. Now, really good-bye.

BEST REGARDS!
ERWIN

✉

Dr Jacob Greenbaum was another of Erwin's medical colleagues.

Erwin's reference to *Dr Schauer* is a cynical comment on the belief — probably expressed by Joseph Sperling—that marrying a foreigner would be a good way to get out.

The identity of *Ing. Weinmann* is not known. However, Erwin is referring here to the frustrating requirement that only relatives, and not friends, were allowed to provide affidavits at that time. *Ing.* was the abbreviation for the German word for "Engineer". This was a title given to anyone who held an advanced degree in professions other than law or medicine. Max's Master's degree in economics entitled him to be addressed as "Herr Ing. Czerner."

Paula's sister Herma was married to Adolph Schanzer. *Mrs Schanzer* was the widow of one of Adolph's relatives, who had obviously been settled in America for some time before his death. Erwin was clearly dismayed by her use of the word "distant" to describe their relationship.

Mr Froehlich in South Norwalk, Connecticut, was related to Paula's husband, Leopold. Dr Sperling, who was serving his internship in New York, traveled to South Norwalk to see Mr Froehlich and solicit his help. The doctor was unsuccessful.

✉

Letter 4   Prikope 35
From Paula   Prague
                              June 29, 1939

My Dearest Children,

Now you are already in the USA and I give you my heartiest wishes and congratulate you. No matter how sad I am inside, I am glad that you have arrived safely. I could not really expect to have a letter from you yet, but please write as soon as possible and in detail about your trip, how you are, and about sweet little Tommy. The children are very well behaved, even Raya! You would hardly recognize Rayushka now. She is not so stubborn and angry any more, and has temper tantrums very rarely. She is happy when I compliment her, and then she is adorable. Helgichka acts very grown-up. I believe they have grown, as one can see by their clothes, and they have both gained weight. Under my care Helga has gone from 20 kg to 21 kg, and Raya weighs 17 kg. So you know they are well and you can have peace of mind. They also look very well — I see that they get in the sun. Elisha picked them up and took them for a walk, which was very welcomed by me, and yesterday they were with Regina.

During our move Faninka will take them because the Wolffs are away in Radovice. Hella and Gertrude are at Karl's. Tante Elsa will be back on Sunday and she also is willing to have them [the children], but at Rabl and Faninka's there's more room for them and they would be closer to me. We move on the 8th. Over Saturday and Sunday the office will be furnished and it is possible that patients could come on Monday. Mrs Wolff telephoned and asked me to bring the children to her for a day because she would like to see them. I told her that it's too far for me and for her it would be too complicated, because the maid has no time to get them and she doesn't either. We went back and forth about it. The children could visit her for lunch sometime before they leave, that would be better for me. Moshko's mother was here and is, thank God, well. She feels well and peppy.

Now I will let the children write something, then they'll have their snack and I'll take them out. Dear Helga is, thank God, such a lovely child. Darling Rayushka gives me a lot of trouble about eating. If you could see them, you would be glad to see how well they look and how good their spirits are and that they are not afraid.

And now, greetings and kisses from my heart and I embrace each of you,

Your Mama, who loves you

Regina, as noted, was Armin's wife.

The *Wolffs, Kathe and Rolf,* were Max and Irma's closest friends. Irma and Kathe went together to a couturier to have clothes especially made to wear in America. They promised each other that neither would wear her new things until she got to the U.S. The Wolffs were not able to emigrate and eventually perished along with their daughter

Marion, a playmate of Helga's and Raya's.

Gertrude was the teenage daughter of Elisha and Hella.

Karl was another of Max's brothers. He was married to a Gentile whose family, the Poppers, were friends of Max and Irma. Karl succeeded in emigrating to New York, but committed suicide in 1946 by jumping from a window.

The *Rabls*, Julius and Faninka, were relatives of Paula's husband, Leopold Froehlich. They had a house in Zbraslav (also called Konigsberg), where the children liked to visit.

✉

Letter 5
From Erwin

Prikope 35
Prague
June 29, 1939

DEAR MOSHKO AND IMSHKO:

I sent a telegram to you yesterday and I hope you understood it. Mr Posin has received his U.S. visa and he is willing to take the children along. The consul informed him that he would be allowed to take them along only if you, dear Moshko, were waiting for them in Holland. They cannot be taken to the USA except with you – they would not be permitted to land. They can get into the USA under the Russian quota only if they are with you. But since the consul knows, through Mr Weiss, that you did not wait in Holland but are already in New York, he cannot legally issue a visa, because if they are alone, they would come under the Czech quota, and as Ingles and Miss Brand have advised, they could qualify for the Czech preferential visa only if you apply for Form 575 in Washington. How long this would take I do not know as yet. Should the matter of the children succeed through Mrs Sharp in the next few days, then they could come in September. The third possibility, to bring them to the USA more quickly, would be for you, dear Moshko – and no one else, not even Irma – to come back to Holland; then someone could be found to take them to The Hague and they could get visas immediately. I must leave that decision to you. Anyway, they are well off here and maybe it is not necessary to hurry things up if it doesn't go any other way. But they will have to say good-bye to Tante Steffi, who may not want to let them leave; however the road may be easier for children. Naturally, we will try other ways to hasten the trip for H. and R., but what I'm writing you today is the situation as it exists since yesterday. And today is a holiday, so nothing more can be done today. I will inform you as soon as I hear more favorable news.

There is a lot of work for us to do because of the forced changes here regarding living and practice ("Neuerichtung").

Mr Sharp reported that in London in Bloomsbury House, I am registered with four hundred other Czech doctors. Chances there are minimal, however. But I got a letter that I might be accepted. Sharp recommended Chile but 1200 pesos are necessary (about 1200 Swiss francs) for landing money, and he gave me the address of a Miss Marie Ginsberg, Geneva, whom I have written. I got a letter from Dr Sperling in which he recommends a doctor in Leeds whom he does not know personally and he recommends that I write him because he might be willing to guarantee the English permit, and in addition I had an invitation from a man in England through Sperling. So these are all the plans.

It is impossible to express how much work and worry dear Mother has – and unfortunately at this time we have the worst household help we have ever had.

Your mother's injury, dear Moshko, is almost healed and everything is all right.

CORDIAL REGARDS AND KISSES,
ERWIN

✉

The identity of *Mr Weiss* is not known;
Miss Brand was with the U.S. consulate

in Prague, and probably *Ingles* was as well.

Mrs Sharp was undoubtedly the wife of the Reverend Sharp who ran the emigration mission.

Irma could not get visas for the children because she was technically a stateless person in Czechoslovakia. When she married Max, a Russian national, she lost her Czech citizenship. The Froehlichs had been opposed to this marriage partly for this reason; they also felt that she was marrying beneath her. Ironically, it was her marriage to a Russian national that provided her entry to the U.S. and saved her life.

Neurichtung were the new laws concerning Jews.

Bloomsbury House was a former hotel in the Bloomsbury section of London; it was taken over by various organizations which were trying to arrange emigration for European victims of Nazi oppression.

✉

Letter 6
From Paula

Masna Street 19
Prague
July 19, 1939

MY CHERISHED AND BELOVED CHILDREN,

If you knew how often I think of you, you wouldn't be annoyed because I write so rarely. It seems like an eternity since you left us and my thoughts are with you always. I am constantly distracted, and as long as I have my little girls here I find comfort from them and I mustn't think of their departure. However, they belong to you and I am allowed to enjoy them while they are here. – and then I will stay behind with dear Erwin and we will live our lonesome life. I hope only that God will make everything turn out all right. Why did we have to separate? How nice it would be if I could travel to you. Whether my wishes and dreams will be fulfilled, all of us being again together ... I can't tell you how much I enjoy your news and that you, thank God, are all right so far. If I get good news from you, I find satisfaction. All I wish and pray to God for are health and happiness for my children and for the whole family and the Jewish people.

I would like to know how you have gone about getting settled in your little nest. Is the apartment nice, and how do you do your housekeeping? I would love to have a glimpse! We are quite satisfied with our apartment, although it is not in order yet, and I have a good feeling about it. You probably know what I'm thinking. Again, if only I could have the little children here and know you are well settled and that you, dear Moshko, are firmly established.

I am worried enough about Erwin, but if God wills it, he will also be safe. About the little children — don't worry about them, they are healthy, thank God. Dear Helgichka gained two kg and Rayushka gained one kg. If Rayushka wasn't so stubborn, she could gain more weight too! You will be pleased when you see them again. Today I was with Elisha in Rubesova [Street] but Dr Wesley was not there, she had an auto accident, so we spoke to someone else. Elisha will write details. They [the children] will be with us until August 28, and my worry will be relieved then when I know they will be well taken care of because Armin will be waiting for them in England. He left today with Regi and he will take care of them till you arrive. Saying good-bye will be difficult for us and I wish you a happy reunion and a hundred years of togetherness.

The Rabls were very nice and they had the children with them for four days. Sunday we were in Konigsberg from 8:30 until evening and the children swam in the Moldau and got a nice tan. Faninka [Rabl] hoped that the children could come there more often. Every day she comes to see them and enjoys them and they like her. I had a maid, but the children didn't like her and we had to find someone else. The children are always outside and are the center of attention. Everyone likes them.

Greetings and kisses to you and to Janko and perhaps I'll write you more tomorrow.

MAMA

✉

The British Chadwich Commission was planning a project to take Jewish children by ship to England. The Commission's Prague headquarters were in Rubesova Street. The Froehlichs habitually referred to this emigration project, for which Helga and Raya were registered, as the "Rubesova" project. Dr Wesley was probably a Commission worker.

Konigsberg was the German name for Zbraslav, where the Rabls lived.

Janko ["Jack"] Czerner was Max's oldest brother who had settled in New York several years earlier. Max and Irma stayed with him and his wife, Ann, in New York immediately upon arrival but after a few days Max left Irma there with Tommy and went on alone to St. Louis to begin his new job with Shell Oil and look for an apartment.

In July, 1939, the Zentralstelle für Jüdische Auswandering *(Central Office for Jewish Emigration) was set up in Prague under the direct supervision of Adolph Eichmann. In that same month, Jewish students were excluded from German language public schools in the Protectorate.*

✉

Letter 7   Masna Street 19
From Erwin   Prague
                                                              July 28, 1939

DEAR IRMA AND MOSHKO:

We received your letter with the three pictures of Tommy yesterday and I see from that letter that you have decided to wait for the preferential visas rather than have Max go to England. If this worked, it would naturally be better if the children could be taken to New York by someone else — Elisha, for instance. "Both roads run at the same time": that is, if the matter is resolved in Washington and Prague is notified, the children will immediately get their visas and be able to go; on the other hand, a card arrived just now from London from Armin that Herr Adler gave the guarantees for the children and that arrangements have already been made at Bloomsbury House, so the possibility exists that they could be taken along in August with the action of the Rubesova — that they would go to England to Armin and later be taken to Moshko. Therefore, whatever can be done soonest will be done, depending on what decision you make.

The children are very well — they are lively and well-nourished — but sometimes they can, especially Raya, be quite difficult but in general are very well-behaved. They go for walks with Mama or sometimes with Rablichek or Faninka. Today, for a change, they went with Hedy who is still waiting for the permit to go to England. Otherwise, none of the other relatives seems to take an interest in them — I am particularly annoyed about this, especially at Hella who never appeared. Yesterday the children went with Grandmother Czerner for a walk in the afternoon. Uncle Rudolph came here for the first time to take a look at our apartment and he sends his regards.

About me, nothing new. I'm trying to keep my balance, in spite of the fact that I have written to all possible countries and am as discouraged and worried as I was last September. That means I have nothing tangible except for "possibilities" about which I have written Dr Sperling in detail, and there have been no developments in the meantime. I have no news as to whether I would be permitted to take the exam in England and to practice. If that falls through, I have no guarantor for a temporary stay. As far as the USA, is concerned there is now a waiting period of three years. Frau Schanzer's affidavit is only good for six months. We need the affidavit from Mr Froehlich in South Norwalk because Mama has none. But Mr Froehlich hasn't answered, just like the guarantor in Leeds whom Dr Sperling recommended. That means I will land where the wind will blow me – and then what? To wait for five years for citizenship, and then who knows what difficulties will arise? I have had no news from Chile since Genff gave me the happy news about my supposed admission to England. An ad in the paper would be indicated because I want to leave no stone unturned – however, I don't expect much from this. I was made a member of the Graphology Association in Paris.

July 29. Today I spoke on the phone with Armin. He needs a copy of your affidavit by Tuesday at the latest for Bloomsbury House – or a copy of the USA visa. First thing this morning I went to the US consulate. They weren't too cooperative at first and Miss Brand said if the children go to England, they can't get the USA visa here but only in England. They would give the children the visa only if Moshko is in

London and if the U.S. consul in London telegraphs to the U.S. consulate in Prague that Moshko is actually in England. So things are more complicated again. Therefore I have requested your affidavit from Miss Brand whichever way things go. Armin told me that if the copy of the affidavit does not arrive in England by Tuesday at the latest, then the children cannot travel to England in August but will have to wait two months. I received the affidavit today, Saturday noon. Unfortunately it is a weekend but with considerable bribes I have succeeded in getting the photostat promised by Monday morning so that Armin could get it by Tuesday by air mail. I will give Armin all this new information. Otherwise, we are busy with all sorts of formalities (signatures, etc.) — not only for those who are emigrating. The practice is, as usual, bad. Every day I have an English lesson.

GREETINGS AND KISSES,
ERWIN

✉

Herr Adler was Armin's employer, a well-known furrier who had emigrated to England.

Hedy was Hedy Schanzer Bock, daughter of Paula's sister Herma and Irma's first cousin who went to England and then to New York. Not much is known about Hedy except that she was one of the first women in Prague to undergo cosmetic rhinoplasty.

Hella, as noted above, was Elisha's wife.

Uncle Rudolph was Paula's only brother.

Graphology (the study of handwriting for the purposes of character analysis) was one of Erwin's many passionate hobbies.

Letter 8

1939

Dear Mommy and Daddy,

I weighed myself at Grandma's and I weigh 21 kg dressed and 20 kg undressed. We are fine at Grandma's. We eat very much — I am already a little bigger, and Raya is too. All of our clothes are too small. We eat lots of fruit — peaches, strawberries, gooseberries, cherries, apricots and we eat fruit.

Helga

Letter 9

Dear Mommy and Daddy,

I'm so glad we will see you soon. Can Tommy walk yet? Grandma already has a new apartment, it is nice. For now we are at the Rabls' they took us to Zbraslav from morning to night. We went swimming there, and went on the swings. Raya is always with Mr Rabl. We stayed at Zbraslav from morning to night. We had a very nice time.

Helga

Letter 10

(I am guiding Raya's hand)

Dear Mommy and Daddy,

We ran in front of the house in Zbraslav at the Rabls' house and we went swimming.

Raya

Letter 11

Dear Mommy and Daddy,

I am an assistant in my uncle's office and I am fine at Grandma's house. Mommy, when I heard you speak on the telephone, we started to cry with Grandmother.

Helga and Raya

Letter 12　　　　　　　　　　　　　　　Masna Street 19
From Paula　　　　　　　　　　　　　　　　　　Prague
　　　　　　　　　　　　　　　　　July or August, 1939

MY DEAREST CHILDREN,

　　　We are happy with your letter and with the pictures.
Tomichek is beautifully fat. I couldn't look at it enough —
neither could the girls. And you dear Shishinko, you look well
too. Now, dear Shishinko, you are alone without Moshko —
how long will that last? And if the trip is successful, I expect you
will move. The darling girls are, thank God, lively and robust,
particularly Helga. She has changed very much. She has, thank
God, grown and is a whole head taller than Raya. Raya also
grew but she doesn't eat as much as Helgichka. Monday or
Tuesday I'll go with the dear children to Schary, to see if she
can speed up the trip and, in general, give us a hand. I would
love to have the children for another year. If they were with you
now you would have more work. But unfortunately, one cannot
plan and every day there is something else. Thank God you are
already out. I hope dear Erwin will also be successful in leaving.
Everybody promises and paints everything in beautiful colors,
but it is very difficult now to do anything. But I don't want to
cry on your shoulder. I hope God doesn't abandon us.

　　　Now I think Elisha will come to you and I would be
happy if he could take them [the children] along so they don't
have to travel with strangers. And, dear Moshko, it would save
you the trip [to England]. We hope for the best and wish they
were already there, even though that's hard for me to even think
about. They are very happy with us and they don't even want
to go. And they ask if we could go along with them, and

Helgichka writes us a visa and that's that! She listens when we discuss it. When Rayushka hears that name [Elisha] she doesn't want to hear about it and changes the subject. She gets really angry for a moment — but then gets very good again. Helgichka is more understanding. Sometimes I would like to eat her up! It doesn't do you any harm to have only Tomichek for awhile, so you have more peace and quiet to arrange everything before the girls come. I'd love to see how you cook and keep house — but I know you are practical and you know how to take care of things.

Irma was "alone without" Max because he went to St Louis to see about getting an executive job with Shell Oil. If his trip is successful, Paula says, then Irma will move with him to St Louis.

The identity of *Schary* is not known.

Letter 13

August 1, 1939

DEAR MOMMY AND DADDY

We will soon come. I already miss you. Uncle Erwin is very nice and Grandma too.

MANY KISSES,
HELGA

Letter 14

[Erwin guiding her hand]

DEAR MOMMY AND DADDY,

Today the clouds made peepee. Erwin is very adorable and Grandma has a lot of work. We have a new maid. So now we've written more than Helga — hee hee hee.

There is a white doctor's coat hanging over there. That's enough.

RAYA

Letter 15   Masna Street 19
From Erwin   Prague
                                              August 5, 1939

DEAR MOSHKO AND IMSHKO,

Today dear Mama has written a lot and I shall only report the essentials in order to get this letter mailed quickly. Since new difficulties have arisen and it is not yet clear when and with whom the children can leave, it is best to wait until the consulate here gets the news from the USA that the preferential visa has been granted. When it arrives, the children will travel with Elisha or Karl or others. To date there is no news from the consulate and I was told to inquire again after three days. There is already a permit in England, Armin writes, but since the timing isn't right, it is better to choose the route of the preferential visa and wait. And since the whole process may be delayed by Tante Steffi, it makes no sense to send telegrams before one is sure. One cannot count on anything and I would be uneasy about you waiting in England not knowing when the children would arrive. I also wait, above all, for a preferential visa although the children are registered for the England option in the Rubesova project. Believe me, with the best of information no one can figure out when and how the children will travel and certainly not on which ship, but they will go as soon as possible. I have had another disappointment: I am not on the list of fifty doctors to be admitted to England. Apparently preference is given to married doctors. My best chance is gone.

HEARTFELT GREETINGS AND LOVE FROM,
ERWIN

✉

Tante Steffi, as noted above, was a code name for the Nazis.

On August 5, 1939, the first laws were issued to isolate Jews from the non-Jewish population. Certain restaurants were marked off-limits to Jews; others were allowed to serve them only in separate rooms. Swimming and bathing areas were also marked off-limits. Jewish patients in hospitals and nursing homes were segregated too. Jews who entered any restricted areas were punished.

✉

Letter 16   Masna Street 19
From Erwin   Prague
                                      August 9, 1939

DEAR IRMA AND MOSHKO,

Most of all, dear Moshko, I congratulate you on your job. I'm sure it is amazing how fast you got it and that you also established personal contact with the bosses so quickly. I'm sure you'll have a big career there. So you have the same boss, Shell, again — and the same department, Asphalt. I hope life in St. Louis will be better than New York. And now to answer your questions:

(1) So far I have not yet heard from the U.S. consulate that the preferential visa was granted. I go there every day and every day they say it will come. As soon as I get it for the children, as soon as I have it in my hand, I'll send a telegram. Whom they will go with is secondary. With Elisha, if they are ready by August 15 — but it is not sure whether Elisha will have an exit permit for this date. For the time being it is only promised — so it is possible they could go with him later too. And if not, then maybe with Karl at the end of September. I will tell you in the next letter whether the Sharps would take the children along — they're not in Prague now but they'll be back. But as I said, all depends on getting the preferential visa.

(2) Today a note from the Chadwich Committee: Helga and Raya are on the list that arrived from London. As far as we know, the group will leave at the end of the month. We'll get further details. Moshko would have to arrange to be in London before the children's arrival so he could get the visa for them in

London, and he would have to know the ship. It could happen that this Children's Group would leave later. That happened in another case, that's why they give the date tentatively. Therefore, you, Moshko, may sit unnecessarily in England – the expected ship might leave without the children and then what? This could easily happen, because here you can't even count on the time, not even on the same day! Naturally, the Rubesova [project] would have a big advantage because it would be easier for a large group of children to leave since each child doesn't have to have separate documents. There are so many arrangements to be made, though, it might be hard to link up. It's also so late, so it's better to wait for the preferential visa because it could come any day. So wait patiently. The main thing is that the children are well and are often in the fresh air. They eat enough and have a good time.

(3) Bosch: you already paid for a month's storage in Hamburg. You still owe for a second month, which was not billed. We can't pay that from here, it has to be paid in New York in dollars.

(4) The children will get the visa [illegible] the other way around: as soon as the visa gets to the consulate in Prague.

(5) Mah jong [code?] is here and we'll send it along with the children.

(6) Mother has no affidavit, she has only been registered since January 1939. I have an affidavit from Frau Schanzer that is valid for half a year but it can be renewed.

(7) All the plans for my travel to London are nil so far – I wrote you that in the last letter and also to Dr Sperling.

Sunday we were at Rabls' with the children in Zbraslav for the whole day and when we returned we found your letter.

In order to get a letter to the *Clipper* [air mail] one has to mail it either on Monday or on Thursday.

HEARTFELT GREETINGS,

ERWIN

✉

Bosch was the person handling the details of the storage of household goods that Max and Irma had managed to ship out of Prague to Hamburg in the early days of the Occupation, and later to New York. A friendly German officer had turned his back and allowed them — against all regulations — to pack a van with most of their possessions before they gave up their luxury apartment and left Prague. Helga and Raya still have some of the furniture, dishes, photograph albums — even pots and pans — from Prague.

From March 15 to early June of 1939, it was relatively easy to get exit permits and take personal property out of the country, even valuable property. But with the issuance of an edict on June 23, 1939, after the establishment of the *Zentralstelle*, things became much more difficult. In November an emigration tax was imposed if the value of the property exceeded 200,000 crowns or if the applicant's taxable income in 1938 was at least 140,000 crowns. The tax rate was not less than 25% of the net value of the property, collected by Protectorate authorities. In March 1940, a separate "Jewish tax" was imposed, to be collected by the *Zentralstelle*, although in January 1940 local tax offices were authorized to issue tax waivers when they thought it necessary.

Apart from anything else, the preparations for emigration were complicated and demoralizing – they constituted a kind of cat-and-mouse game. Once the would-be émigré had found a country willing to issue him an entry visa, he had to type out six copies each of sixteen forms, on which all questions had to be answered in full, whether applicable or not. In addition to these forms, the applicant had to supply three photographs, his birth and marriage certificates, proof of his local citizenship, a character reference that could not be more than six weeks old, official municipal proof of his place of residence, and both tax receipts and a Treasury certificate attesting to the payment of all taxes. He had to provide a list of his real estate and jewelry; these possessions were transferred irrevocably to the Germans. A second list was required documenting all the possessions he wished to take with him. This second list — which could include furniture, household goods, furs, carpets, books, etc. — had to be accompanied by official appraisals of this property's value. Possessions taken out of the country could be taxed at 100% of these appraisals.

While people were working frantically to prepare these mountains of paperwork, visas and other dated documents expired. Local officials of foreign governments refused to renew the visas.

When all the documents were finally completed, the file was taken to the *Zentrastelle* where, in the basement, workers from the Jewish Community went over the papers to make sure that there was nothing in them that would enrage the Germans and destroy the plans of the applicant, who was understandably a nervous wreck. From the basement, the applicant went into the main hall to be interviewed by various officials, each in his own cubicle. The last stop was the first floor where SS men figured the emigration tax.

About three weeks later, the applicant, now virtually destitute, was called back to the *Zentralstelle* to get his exit visa. In addition, at that time he was often met with a demand for an additional payment that could run to twenty, thirty or even fifty thousand crowns, depending on the mood of the Nazi official.

After the outbreak of war between Germany and the Soviet Union in June of 1941, emigration became even more difficult; it virtually ended when deportations started in October 1941 to Lodz. War with the United States was declared two months later.

✉

To Prague

Letter 17   Statler Hotel
From Max   St. Louis
                                                                August 20, 1939

Dear Mama and Erwin,

Dear Irma sent me your letters from New York and I thank you for them and for all the love you give to the children. Today I received your telegram that the children will leave Tuesday with Elisha and Thursday, with God's help, will board the boat and we were overjoyed — I don't need to tell you just how much. And I know that you are glad too, even though you will find it difficult to give up the children after these months with them, but with God's help you will see them soon again. Maybe there was a good reason for the children not leaving along with us. Perhaps they were better off with you than they would have been here with us in the first few chaotic months. But it was difficult for us to be away from them. By the time you read this letter, maybe the children will already be with us, and they will be telling us about Babichka and Streichek [Uncle] and the grandmother who doesn't speak Czech very well [Max's mother] and about Rablichek and all the others, and we are grateful to you for being so good to the little ones. If only they were here already. We read so much here about Europe in the newspapers, we don't know what to think and believe. I only think that nobody wants war, and I have an unshakeable faith that there will be peace. And I hope that we all see each other soon. Whatever we can do from here, we will do.

During the short time I have been here I have established the necessary connections — even though some of them are on vacation during the hot summer weather. But at the beginning of September, in approximately two weeks, they'll all return.

For you, Erwin, I don't want to raise false hopes and make wild plans. My letters will be brief – and I hope I'll send you only concrete telegrams. And when that isn't possible, I'll write you only facts – that means, when the plans come to fruition. You will probably say that a miracle is required – but I do believe in miracles, and many miracles have already occurred. Any of our hopes that materialize are miracles – and I hope all of our hopes will become realities! For the moment I have some connections with presidents of committees in hospitals, but the rest will take longer.

First, something that could speed things up: I heard at last from Franz Fleischmann. His address: François Fleischmann, 97 Blvd de la Reins, Versailles, France. I found out that there is a firm that at the moment is interested in your specialty, and I wrote him. You already know that Fleischmann is reliable, helpful and generous. And besides that, he owes me for my help with his wife and child, as he mentioned. He will write you, and I gave him your new address. But for good measure you could write him too. I wrote him that you will stay with him temporarily and that you urgently want to come to us. For reference, I gave him the address of Paul Froehlich whom you wrote after our visit with Uncle Alois – today you can't get any job without references. You will hear more from him – and from us – and I will hear from both of you.

In regard to Mother, send me the dates again for another affidavit. To send an affidavit now is useless, because Mother will not leave without you and the quota takes so long that one has to renew the affidavit at least twice. But send the data anyway — including the date and number of the registration. However, that's the least of our worries. As soon as the affidavit is all that's necessary, all you have to do is send me a telegram.

To you, dear Mama, special thanks. I know you trust me as if you were my own mother and I tell you both in one breath, just as I tell Erwin and my brothers and sisters, I won't disappoint you. Whatever is in my power I will be happy to do. You, dear Mama, sense this — but I want to make it perfectly clear to Erwin. I know that you sometimes doubt it, Erwin. But I see by your devotion to the children that you don't feel bitterness toward me either. And I promise you that I will leave no stone unturned to help you. You say that Karl will be leaving in a few weeks. Then my mother and Lotte and Ettel will be left behind. I could easily get affidavits for them, but I don't know how things are with Lotte — Sperling speaks with Irma occasionally and I'm sure Irma writes you about that. I think that in spite of his best intentions he won't be able to do much in the very near future. The normal way is long. But don't break off the correspondence — *you never can tell* [in English]. And now, don't worry too much. Most important: try to stay well, health is your greatest asset. God has helped very much already and He will help again. Send a picture sometime. Best to all relatives and friends. Stay together. Are they all still there? Sincere greetings and kisses. My thoughts are with you.

Moshko

✉

Franz [Franta] Fleischmann was a Czech colleague of Max's at Shell in Prague. He emigrated to Paris where he was joined by his wife and daughter; the three of them eventually moved to London.

Paul Froehlich, Irma's cousin, emigrated to Bogotá, Colombia. His father, *Uncle Alois*, was a step-brother of Paula's husband, Leopold Froehlich.

Ettel was Max's eldest sister who lived with his mother. She did not survive. The reference to Lotte is probably to her health, which could exclude her from the U.S.

On August 11, 1939, Jews living in the provinces of the Protectorate were ordered to resettle in Prague within one year.

✉

Letter 18
From Paula

Masna Street 19
Prague
August 21, 1939

MY DEAREST CHILDREN AND TOMICHEK,

We were very happy with your letter. I would love to write you every day so you could know everything, but the day is so full that I have only the evenings to write. In the evenings I have to tell the little girls stories, and the last few evenings the Broks were here because of the girls so I couldn't write then either. In addition, it takes so very long for our letters to reach you. The thought of the enormous distance between us hurts my heart, but I'm glad that I know that you are well. But Shishinko, take care of yourself, don't overdo it. Thank God you have moved and furnished, and when the girls get there it will mean even more work, but I know Moshko helps you. Thank goodness you are making a living. Everybody envies me and says I must be so happy — my darling Shishinko. I would like to help you and have you all around me again — like a mother duck. The distance is a bad thing, it makes one very nostalgic. With God's help we'll be together again. We can't allow ourselves to lose hope. And when your children are with you again I'll be content. I hope you'll find enough friends. My daily prayer is that everything should turn out all right.

Tomichek seems to be very lively. Dear Helgichka tells me she wants to feed him by herself and take him for walks alone but Rayushka doesn't want to give in on that and then they quarrel. Helgichka is very sensible and very good. Dear Raya is still a little child but she's good too. She steals my heart (*hertzgoniff*). Everybody loves her and fusses over both of them.

Today we had a visit from Kathe Wolff and she says they look very well and that they've grown. She wants to take them for lunch on Wednesday. I ran into Slonitz-Hirsch on Wenceslaus Square, and she sends her regards. Do you have a park nearby? Do you have a pram for Tomichek? How do you communicate with people? What kinds of food do you eat? Can you cook Czech style, or are you adapting to customs over there? Can you get smoked meat? The children say that's what they would miss most. Do you get poultry? I'm sure you don't bother to cook for yourself, only for Tomichek. Is it very expensive there?

About us here, Helgichka will tell you everything. She is very observant, doesn't miss a thing — she is the light of my life. She is a big girl already — so polite and understanding. We received the letter from Moshko, typewritten, to which you added — I'm sorry you have to spend so much on stamps and that little dumpling [Tomichek] won't leave you alone. How do you make yourself understood?

The children say, "We will write a visa for you, and you and Uncle Erwin will be able to come with us and we will speak for you and take care of you when we go places." We will miss them very much. But even so, I hope to God they will soon be with you. Yesterday we were in Konigsberg again — they like it there very much, in the fresh air, and going swimming. You should see them splashing in the water — it's a pleasure to watch them. How is it there with household help? I thought I had a winner with my Marya, but in the evening she ran off and she's no better than all the others.

Now I'll go to sleep. I have to turn down my bed, the girl didn't come back, but one has to put up with that. Who knows if she'll stay? Erwin received a letter from Sperling, saying the same things about Froehlich and Schanzer. Hedy is in London. A young man came today and he said that Dr Sperling is a waiter! Is that possible? I can't believe it! Write me whether this is really so. Unfortunately, now there are bad times everywhere. Thank God you're better off. Here I'm so worried about the future—but I don't want to give you a heavy heart. But you do know how I feel for you. And even though it's very hard for me, I wish the girls were already with you. Today Dr Slonitz was here to visit Erwin. She picked up some [documents] that she wants to copy. The children went to visit Aunt Elsa — we ran into them on the [Boulevard] Prikope.

And now the most important thing — Erwin did not want to send you a telegram as long as there was nothing definite. Moshko always wants telegrams, and Erwin wants to send only facts. Even Armin urged him to send a telegram. On Monday there should be a decision, and we don't want to give you false hope, so listen — Armin called wanting to speak to Erwin but Erwin was out shopping. Then we got a telegram from Armin telling Erwin to call him. The upshot was that the children would leave on the 30th with the Rubesova [group]. But on Monday Elisha arranged things for them and on Tuesday they can go with Elisha directly. In any case, the Rubesova have not left yet so that remains a last resort. Armin definitely wanted Erwin to wire you that the children would board a boat in Hamburg on the 24th. All day Monday I was with the children and Elisha at Tante Steffi's. Today (Tuesday) Tante Steffi gave the children trouble so they cannot leave this week. If we had given in and sent all those telegrams you would have gotten your hopes up for nothing. To tell you the truth, Armin didn't care at all about the children. He saw them once in two weeks, and

Regina came only twice. Armin said, I won't take the children until I go or I'll wait for them there. Elisha does all the paper work and he also confers with Erwin. Erwin urged Armin to do something because Erwin had to be in his office and couldn't do it all. Elisha had more time for this — and he's also a good actor. He did everything well. Tomorrow we have to go back there to German Headquarters. It's better for Elisha to go there with them. When they reach Hamburg, they'll wire you. So, be happy. Maybe they'll get there before this letter does, because air-mail usually takes ten to fourteen days. We got two letters from you at once — one took ten days, the other two weeks. About the matter with Bosch, Erwin took care of it. Aunt Malva was here today. Write again very soon: good news, that you are well.

KISSES AND GREETINGS FROM
MAMA

Best regards to Janko and family. Many thanks for being so good to Shisha.

✉

Edith Slonitz-Hirsch was a close friend of Irma's and a medical colleague of Erwin's; she and Erwin were the same age. She was Helga and Raya's pediatrician. She did not survive.

Konigsberg was the German name for Zbraslav. It was actually an old German name for the town — a name that was resurrected by the Nazis.

Paula's complaint about having to "put up with" turning down her own bed obviously reflects the comfortable life she had been leading. Her husband, Leopold, and his brothers owned a candy and liqueur factory. Leopold died of a heart attack in 1936.

The "same things" that Dr Sperling and, evidently, Max and Irma had been saying about "Schanzer and Froehlich" were probably expressions of disappointment in the response of these two American relatives to requests for help. It does appear that Mrs Schanzer signed an affidavit since she referred in it to Erwin as "a distant relative" of her late husband. But Mr Froehlich in Connecticut did not help.

Despite Paula's statement that "Armin didn't care at all about the children", he later proved to be a devoted uncle to the girls.

Elisha was "a good actor" and it was better for him to go to German headquarters with the children because, when he was there he often employed clever ruses. For instance, he surreptitiously pinched Helga to make her cry so that the disturbance would help to move them ahead in line. However, more than once, Raya came fiercely to her sister's defense and embarrassed him by loudly exposing this "child abuse" to everyone within earshot.

Aunt *Malva Schnurmacher* was one of Paula's five sisters: the other four were Rosa Vogl, Herma Schanzer, Clara Hirschl and Elsa Brok.

✉

Letter 19   Masna Street 19
From Erwin   Prague
                                          August 23, 1939 — Evening

DEAR IRMA & MOSHKO,

    Tomorrow I will send you a telegram to tell you that the children will not leave until next week on the 31st. On Saturday I received a telegram from Armin telling me to call him. I did, and he told me that the children should come at all costs to England as soon as possible, even if it should be necessary to pay a companion to take them. I told him that the children's papers are still held up, but on Monday the 21st they are to get their exit permits. On that day they should get their visas and their permits for their clothing and possessions and then they could leave immediately on Tuesday with Elisha. Therefore, the decision will be made on Monday, or Tuesday at the latest, and then I'll send you a telegram immediately. Armin had me send you a telegram on the 19th, well before the decisive Monday, but by now you know that things are still held up. But on Monday, Mama and Elisha and the little ones were at the Bureau for four hours, and after two more hours Elisha got things done. They did not get their visas on Monday after all, but they got them on Tuesday, along with the other permits. Today we were informed that a cabin on the HAPAG [Hamburg-American Passenger Line] was reserved for next week on Thursday, and therefore, as I said, the children will now really go next week from Prague to Hamburg and from there directly to you! So, tomorrow, Rubesova will be definitely cancelled [for the girls], because now they have everything set for a direct journey to you with Elisha. Besides, the Children's Project probably wouldn't leave until the

31st or even later and they wouldn't get to you until much later than that.

And they couldn't go sooner than next Tuesday anyway, even if something happened in between, because the visa for Rubesova is a group visa and then we would have to rush and look for a stranger to accompany them. Today things aren't so simple. *The only possibility, and the most comfortable for the children, and primarily the fastest possibility under the present circumstances, is to send them with Elisha. He waited for them even though he has an exit permit that is reaching the expiration date.* I only hope now that all the papers and the boat reservations are in order and that things remain in order for them to leave on the 29th, and that you will get a telegram from Hamburg saying, "On Board." There would have to be some unforeseen event to prevent their leaving, and Elisha *must* leave because his transit visa will expire.

Though you are disappointed that the children are not on the way yet, the last telegram gave you at least a moment of joy. I didn't want to send that telegram because I knew on Saturday that it might take at least until Tuesday to arrange everything, and that's exactly what happened.

And I don't have the money. It's easy for Armin to say, "Better two telegrams than one." The money is used up, and after the children's departure I will send you a detailed accounting, and I myself must be as thrifty as possible with my own funds. Everything is getting more expensive and at the same time, there is almost no work. And when I do work, half of it is unpaid, a quarter is tremendously underpaid, and a quarter is to be paid "later." As a result, I urgently need to rent out one room. Previously, patients' government health insurance covered at least half of my expenses. The relatives lend me nothing. On the contrary, Aunt Malva wants to collect the small amount we owe her although I am sure she doesn't need it. I am in such difficulties and it is impossible to send each telegram *with answer prepaid*. As an example: last Saturday I had to call Armin and it cost about 150 Kr., and after that a telegram with prepaid answer for 300 Kr., so a total of 450 Kr. — for wrong information, so that today I have to send a new telegram. I know, it's your money, but where shall I get it? I spend for unnecessary things and need hundreds and thousands for important things. Your money is all spent. I got nothing from Armin to date, so I must lay out my own. And if things go on I will soon run out of money so I have no choice but to be very frugal.

I'm neither petty nor stingy, and I would prefer not to write about it at all and to just supplement with my own money and not penny-pinch, but I have to — particularly if no one wants to lend me anything. At the same time, I am trying not to let your expenses get too high. While Elisha is waiting a second week for the children he charges me his expenses and I squeeze him down as much as I can. He demands his money without asking where I get it from — it simply has to be here. Because I know that I must not spare expenses to get the children out, I try to control him.

And another word about telegrams: your telegrams arrive mostly at night and they awaken Mama — who, at her age, has to work harder than ever before in the daytime — and then she can't get back to sleep. What sense is there to receive a telegram at one a.m.: "Telegraph Immediately Mother Desperate." etc. Effect: a sleepless night, and getting up at six a.m. to get the children ready for a trip to Zbraslav at seven a.m. And in fact, despite the best intentions, we can't answer those questions — that is, we can't give you an immediate answer. All the things that are necessary to do, as Elisha will soon tell you, are so different from when you were here. You know Elisha. And it is true that Armin, in Prague, didn't do anything for the children — not a single thing. Only when he was already in London he "did what he could," as he wrote me — namely to register in Bloomsbury and make a few phone calls. It's also true that Erwin [he is referring to himself] was only at the consulate once, he sent telegrams and nothing else. That's also the only thing he promised, because, according to Moshko, Elisha should be doing all the leg-work and I [Erwin] should only advise and direct him. Because I sit in my office all the time and have to make house-calls, and you, Moshko, didn't want to inconvenience me by asking me to go to various Bureaus to sit four and five hours at a time, Elisha will claim that he did everything himself. He will tell you how difficult it was for him to arrange and manage everything, and what an invaluable service he did and how he took everything on himself — you should take that with a grain of salt. Moshko already did a lot for him, and will probably do more. He will tell you he did some things only for the children which he actually did for himself. He made a charge of 250 Kr. which he said was for the children but was actually for himself. No matter what, though, he should only bring you your children as soon as possible and they should leave on the thirtieth.

Here too it is very hot. This afternoon Mama and the children went with Uncle Rudolph in the car to Radovice to Tante Rosa. But the children are looking forward to going again on Sunday to the Rabls in Zbraslav. Last Sunday we were there, and all of us went to the highest hill to look for mushrooms; Helgichka has a sharp eye for them.

I got an offer from a man in London (after my last letter to Sperling) to get me a visa for Chile. It would cost about 40 pounds. I didn't answer him yet because now I don't know what is what. As you know, Tante Steffi won't let me out at the moment. Herr Froehlich was named as a relative of Mama's by the Committee of Jewish Women and I asked him for an affidavit but I have not received an answer. I found the name and address of a colleague in my field in St. Louis in my notebook and I made a note of it; it is Horace W. Soper. Aside from that, I know nothing about him. The day before yesterday I received a letter from Sperling, dated August 8. By registered mail I sent him photostats of all my medical documents and in the next few days two more photostats about my gastroscopic activity; and a more extensive *curriculum vitae*.

HEARTFELT GREETINGS,

ERWIN

Letter 20   Masna Street 19
From Erwin   Prague
Late August, 1939

DEAR IRMA & MOSHKO,

Mama will tell you what's going on here, because I'm in a hurry. I will only ask you for the following. Since I occasionally see similar advertisements in English-language newspapers, I beg you to place one in one of the more popular newspapers more or less as follows: "Will any kind person help obtain permits for my brother, Czech-Jewish physician, single, 36, well-known as a specialist for Internal Medicine in Prague. Please write....(address) under "personal."

Perhaps this would make some sense because here it is impossible to get a visa for England now temporarily, or for any other country.

HURRIEDLY, WITH MANY THANKS AND GREETINGS,
ERWIN

[P.S.] Or: "Will any kind person give guarantee..."

[P.P.S] Referring to your card of June 11: Herr Tonin called me yesterday. Since there is no person from HAPAG on board who would supervise the children he refused to take them along. To send a telegram now would not make sense since one doesn't know the plans because the children have no visa as yet, nor do the accompanying persons and you know also that everything is dependent on other things, therefore I don't yet know when and with whom they will travel. Naturally I will try everything, through Mr Chadwich as well as Mr Tonin (Sharp hasn't arrived yet.) I'm not subscribing to the English journal, *The Lancet*, because it is too expensive, unless they reduce the subscription price. Tomorrow Elisha is going to Dr Sommer because of the 850 Kr. bill for cleaning the apartment.

CORDIALLY,
Erwin

Herr Tonin was probably another person working to help with emigration.

The meaning of the reference to *Dr Sommer* and the apartment cleaning is not clear. It may be a reference to the Jewish Community.

On September 1, 1939, Germany invaded Poland. Two days later Britain and France declared war on Germany. World War II had begun.

Letter 21 Masna Street 19
From Paula Prague
September 13, 1939

DEAREST CHILDREN AND TOMICHEK:

I am very unhappy that I have had no news from you,
and I don't know whether you will get these few lines. I would
like to hug you and would like to see Tomichek on his first
birthday! Why does it have to be like this? How wonderful it
would be if you were here. Now I still enjoy having the children
here, but they will also have to leave us and perhaps God will see
to it that a time will come when we'll all be together again.
I worry about you, but I know you'll be all right; and I know
you don't need to worry about me. Here, we don't know from
one day to the next what will happen. So far, thank God, we
can get everything we need, so you can relax about the girls.
Erwin plays with them and goes for walks with them. I
sometimes think he overdoes it because he even takes them
when he visits his patients – they wait for him there and then
they go to the park. As far as their going out with Mrs Cohen
is concerned, that hasn't happened for two weeks because she
had no help at home, so she took them into her home for the
whole day. That went well and everyone enjoyed it. Now, it is
very hard to get somebody because I want them to be well cared
for – so it's easier to keep them at home.

But since yesterday, I do have a maid. She is very good
to the children. I wonder whether the dear children really will
leave on the 18th and I only pray to God that they'll be safe and
happily reunited with you. Even so, I will see them off with a
heavy heart. I had a spat with Elisha, because of Hella. He sees

that we have no help here and "Lady Hella" cannot bestir herself to take the children even a little. I was so angry that I blurted it out to him. If it were you, dear Moshko, you wouldn't behave like this — and you would help even if it were difficult. He also wanted 100 Kr. per day for food, and I told him it cost only 30 Kr. But he's charging you 100 Kr.! He says that you have plenty of money. I write you all this because you should know about it, but I'm angry to be paying for Hella to play the "grande dame" — and she owes you everything! I've had it with them. Elisha says, "In Holland we can live well. Shell is everywhere, and Moshko is known." Your dear mother [Moshko] is a hard worker, and she visits us, and is always very pleased to see the children.

How did you furnish, and what kind of apartment do you have? I'm so happy that you are together, and when you have your little daughters there you will be content— I know how hard it is for you to be apart. I wish I already had a note about their happy arrival. Best wishes to Tomichek for his first birthday — and to you all for the New Year, and good health.

Kisses,
Mother

✉

Mrs Cohen was probably a friend of Paula's.

Tomichek was born on September 27, 1938 — the day the Munich Pact was signed.

"The New Year" is Rosh Hashanah, the Jewish New Year which falls in September.

✉

Letter 22   Masna Street 19
From Erwin   Prague
September 13, 1939

DEAR MOSHKO AND IRMA,

First, our very best wishes for the holidays and also for your move. Since nothing has come from you in the mail, I believe this letter also will be delayed in reaching you.

A few days ago we received a letter from you, Moshko, of August 20, in which you were happily anticipating the children's arrival at any moment. Unfortunately, this happiness must have been short-lived since the children are still here with us: well-cared-for, cheerful, plump and healthy and at this moment yelling for their grandma.

It appears that lately no travel possibilities for them have worked out, and maybe that's a good thing. If they had travelled according to the first telegram, they would have boarded the ship at Hamburg having, however, to turn around at sea and be put up at a hotel in Hamburg, without funds, as has become the fate of others. And if they had taken off a week later, after the second telegram, when everything really did seem to be ready, they would have arrived at the border of the Protectorate and perhaps, by some miracle, at Hamburg – then, as you know, there were no longer any ships departing from there. On the other hand by this time they would not even have reached Rotterdam, as there the spaces on board were all taken. Nevertheless, something should work out. It did not work with the gentleman from Shell, either. Regarding the actions taken with respect to the Rubesova project, what Armin maintains in his letter to Elisha is not true – i.e., that I cancelled the children's places.

The children could have gone up to the very last minute and had everything prepared but the event did not take place — which is what I hope Armin confirmed to you — as well as that no children arrived in August or September! In the meantime, Elisha learned that it would be possible for him to leave with the children from Holland, so I have sent you a wire with this in mind. Subsequently, your telegram came and several days later the tickets for the ship arrived. Since spaces on the ship are not yet available, the earliest the children can leave here with Elisha is on the 18th and embark in Rotterdam on the 23rd. Yesterday I gave Elisha an additional 1200 Kr. for travel expenses and as soon as this thing goes ahead without a hitch and the children actually leave, I will let you know by telegram. Only when it's definite! For, as I have already written, I have no more money for useless telegrams which are true for only half a day, as much of it has already been wasted in this fashion. I need to use it for the children for purposes other than originally intended because food is hard to get. And in addition, I have received nothing from Armin, since Uncle Rudolph supposedly doesn't owe him anything. Paul should have written him, and naturally there is no letter from him.

I have to be very careful, since my own money is shrinking. For the children and Elisha I have spent 18,100 Kr. to date, not including the last two telephone conversations with Armin. I keep accurate records so that you can receive all the details. However, if the children cannot leave on the 18th, I cannot continue to support Elisha and his family. I have told him, I cannot do this under any circumstances. And if he, at that time, is no longer the only possible escort for the children, then I also have other things to discuss with him: he thinks himself so irreplaceable, he has really made a sacrifice by waiting for the children, he has been waiting for such a long time — I believe indeed that this was not the only reason for his postponement of his trip, there surely were others — e.g., to sell his furniture — and for that you do not have the moral obligation to support him — as you have done by sending boat tickets for the three of them and by paying everything for them. However, when it is no longer necessary, I must say he does not deserve another penny from you, and his family even less.

Listen to this: Mama, at her age (and in poor health as I needn't remind you) was left all alone to care for a large apartment and professional offices; without household help for two weeks; with the children; with all the other burdens and worries of which you have no idea; and your sister-in-law, "Mrs Nothing," who knew all about it and had nothing to do in Branki but sit around idly, since she no longer had a household there to care for, did not even make the gesture in all these months to take the children for a one-hour walk, and moreover, ran up debts at your expense!! The children, therefore, had two options: to be taken to the Rabls', or go to the home of a patient in Dejvice [a Prague neighborhood] who was willing to take them from nine a.m. to seven p.m. and where they had a good time. Who else would do it? Sometimes they would go with me to the patients', and afterwards take a short walk. After strangers were so nice to them, Aunt Elsa felt obliged to take them for one day. But the main burden fell on Mama, as always; we cannot afford help, even at your expense, not to mention that we do not know when they will be leaving, it could be any day. Armin writes: "Send the children out immediately — perhaps even in care of the conductor." Perhaps he really means "Send my boss's wife's umbrella", which the children were supposed to bring to him — and not the children themselves. In these uncertain times one cannot let small children travel by themselves — as you must agree. Above all, I must tell you: the journey is still very risky, we have a great responsibility for the children here and we're doing everything that can possibly be done so that things go well for them.

For the children, it is not the least bit frightening here; it might be worse elsewhere, and if it is worse somewhere else than at home then that might be frightening, and one does not know what might happen. Many advise under no circumstances send them off. Since you have already sent tickets, I see that you will take the responsibility on yourselves to send the children on the journey all the same — alone, e.g. through Trieste, is out of the question; therefore, with Elisha through Holland when there is a practical possibility for it. From here Mother and I can do nothing except work on it. It is still uncertain in my mind where the greatest risk actually is; you can be sure that I will do only what is best for you and the children. A sensible plan will be carried out to that end no matter whose suggestion it may be. It is laughable that Armin in the aforementioned letter maintains that I have a personal interest in it, such as Elisha does, that the children only travel when I find it convenient; and that I want to claim credit in your eyes as the clever one who got the children to you. It is not the least bit necessary for me to ingratiate myself. It occurs to me that I have already done more for you than you ever could do or have done for me — in fact, you have even worked against me in the past. I am doing everything quite selflessly for the children and I am unaware of any mistakes being made. Unfortunately, the preferential visa came too late to make the connection. You will perhaps say, "If I were there." But 1) you are not here, and 2) you and Armin left, and you only know how it was when you left, and what was true then does not apply now: therefore 3) because it is a different situation, any advice is no longer valid. Yesterday Elisha and the children received an extension of their sailing papers through October 10th.

Please excuse me for not being more pleasant in this letter but everything is true and to the point, and today that is much more important. In regard to the so-called personal interests, I mentioned it only so that I shall not have to react further to this childish rumor. I hope you have received my two airmail letters dated August 25th and 26th. I sent my best thanks to Sperling for Dr Gutheil's vouching for me, it has made me very happy. Now that I am not in the mood to write, I hope that he has also received my second registered letter of August 25.

GREETINGS AND KISSES,

E.

✉

"The gentleman from Shell" refers to attempts on the part of Shell Oil executives to get the children out. (See Appendix, p. 199)

Food was difficult to get at this time because the Nazis were taking everything. Only black market food — grown in the countryside — was available at a high price.

Paul was Paul Porges, Uncle Rudolph's son, who had emigrated to London. He eventually moved to the U.S. and died on Long Island in the 1970s.

"Mrs Nothing" is an obviously derogatory reference to Elisha's wife, Hella.

Erwin's comment that Max had worked against him in the past may be a reference to a situation that arose well before the Occupation, when Erwin wanted to marry a Gentile nurse with whom he had had a long love affair. Max was strongly opposed to this marriage and was instrumental in pressuring Erwin to give up the idea. Max and Erwin had been close friends at university, and in fact, it was Erwin who introduced Max to Irma. An additional strain on the friendship between Max and Erwin may have been caused by the Czerner family's wish that Erwin, in turn, marry Lotte.

In retrospect, marriage to the nurse could have saved Erwin's life because special circumstances existed for Jews married to Gentiles; their fate was delayed until 1944 and 1945, at which time there was a possibility that they could have survived the war. This was the case with three of Irma's first cousins: Uncle Rudolph's son, Franta Porges, and Aunt Malva's two children, Karl Schnurmacher and Aninka Brezak.

Letter 23 [Postcard]   Masna Street 19
From Paula   Prague

MY DEAR CHILDREN,   September 26, 1939

How much pleasure you gave us when you called again! I heard your voices again — but oh, to see you!! I would love to see you again! But when will it happen? It is my only wish that with God's help we will all be together and then we will stay chained together. And also the dear little children, we miss them so much. You can well imagine. All of a sudden it is so empty here and sad. They left Friday night at twelve o'clock. First they slept a little, then they were awakened at ten-thirty and they were happy to be on their way to you. Saturday morning Erwin sent you a telegram that they had left. And so we thought you would not call any more because it costs so much money. The call was expected on Sunday at four-thirty p.m. — so Erwin waited until five-thirty and then he thought you had received the telegram and had changed your mind about calling. But then you called and so I had you all to myself. Although I was so happy to talk to you, I was very sad that dear Erwin missed your call. When he came home at ten p.m. he was so glad that I had talked to you and his eyes were shining with tears. So now I have my sweet little ones constantly on my mind and wish they were already with you. Today Elisha wrote that they are waiting in Munich to board the ship on the 28th or 29th. Please let us know as soon as they arrive because we are worried and wish only to know that they arrived safely. My blessings be with them.

Once more, best wishes on your birthday, dear Shishinko. Enjoy the day pleasantly with your dear ones. In spirit I am with you — be well and happy.

This week it is gloomy again. I hope God will make everything turn out well, and that Erwin will be busy again. You, dear Shishinko, will have plenty of work with the children. Who will help you? Have you taken an apartment yet? Kisses and regards to you and Tomichek — dear little Tomichek will be one year old. Write to us soon again and tell me all about everything you are doing. I'm interested in all of it!

MAMA

✉

Irma's birthday was October 7th.

✉

Letter 24   Masna Street 19
From Erwin   Prague
DEAR IRMA & MOSHKO,   [September 26, 1939]
    Sorry that I could not talk to you, the reason you know from Mother. Today your card, dated Sept. 4, came with the picture of New York Hospital. Now you will have the children there soon. Here, everything is the same. One room will be leased again. I sometimes have a lot of work — then again, a long time with nothing. Now you will have a nice home all together. Warmest regards and for your birthday best wishes and kisses.

ERWIN

P.S. You will hear everything from Elisha, and from the golden children too; they are so bright. I wish I could be at your reunion — or have a picture.

✉

    The children did not sail until late October, as explained earlier in the Background.

✉

Letter 25   Masna Street 19
From Paula   Prague
MY DEAREST CHILDREN,   October 5, 1939

If only you receive this card! If only I had a letter from
you! Every day I wait for it. I'm terribly lonesome for the little
ones, I can't even describe it, and I'd be content if only I knew
they have already arrived. I'm so happy that at least they're on
their way, and that they are cared for on their way by their uncle
Elisha. That's a big relief. You must appreciate that, and it's
thanks to you that it came about. I was so worried. Last week
we went to Rabls'. He gave us some butter and some ham, which
we can't get here in Prague any more. I wanted to pay him for
it, but he gave it to us — and also fourteen eggs. I was very happy
about that, I missed you very much on my birthday, but Erwin
made it a nice day. And your birthday, dear Shishinka, will
be even sadder for me — but the main thing is that you are
well. Now we wait for a letter from you. I wonder if Elisha has
embarked yet? I said goodbye to the girls with a heavy heart,
but one doesn't know what is going to happen here. I would
have loved to go with them. Erwin has work on and off, but one
can't go anywhere. But God will protect us.

MAMA

✉

"One can't go anywhere": this cryptic
comment is a reference to the restrictive
laws against Jews, some of which had
been in effect since August, 1939.

Many laws were not officially codified until as late as 1944. But the date of codification does not identify the actual date the laws were put into effect. Hints of these things appear in the letters from time to time.

All Jews in the Protectorate over the age of six were ordered to wear the yellow Star of David permanently sewn to the left front of all clothing. [September 1, 1941.]

Jews were barred from dining cars and sleeping cars on trains and from traveling by steamboat down the Moldau. [August, 1940] (The Froehlichs had traveled by steamboat to visit the Rabls at Zbraslav.)

Jews could travel only in the second car of streetcars and only in the rear section of the streetcar if the second car had a center door [September 1940.]

Jews were barred from buses. The blind and war veterans were excepted, but they could sit only if all non-Jews were seated. Jews could not ride on trolleys at all. [November, 1941.]

✉

Letter 26
From Paula

Masna Street 19
Prague
November 8, 1939

MY DEAREST AND BELOVED CHILDREN,

Have you been getting all my letters? Last week I got a letter from Moshko from August 8, and a card from you, Shishinko, from September 26th. I can tell you, dear Moshko, that Erwin did not cancel the children's places on the Rubesova project, but at that time *no* children arrived in England. Elisha has probably already told you that those [children's] transports stopped altogether, and we are very happy now that things turned out that way and that they could go with Elisha and be in good hands for the long journey. When the day of the departure of my darling girls came, I had no thought other than the prayer that they would be happily reunited with you. You can't imagine the worry I had — and I know you will also worry until the children arrive, so we'll both worry — you there and I here. I can't wait until I get your telegram When I see children in the street I get so lonesome. Do you have an apartment yet? Who helps you? I miss the children everywhere!

My darling Helgichka and my Rayushka, if you only knew how I miss you. Write me. Helgichka promised to write me. How did you like the boat? Soon we'll see each other again. Do you like the apartment? How do you speak in school? Please write soon.

GRANDMA

Many kisses from your Uncle Erwin.
I am fine and have lots of work now.

[P.S.] Erwin has lots of work now. Rabl is in the hospital — they had to amputate his leg. Erwin went to see him. His children do not know about it. Arnold is still here and I hope everything turns out well.

MAMA

Arnold, Aunt Rosa Vogl's son who had emigrated to America in 1938, went to Hamburg on a trade mission in 1939 and spent some time in Prague before returning to America for good.

Letter 27
From Paula

Masna Street 19
Prague
November 12, 1939

MY DEAREST DARLING CHILDREN,

I don't know if you received all my letters, and I am yearning for one from you. The last word I received, as I've already told you, was a card from October 1st. How I would have loved to witness your reunion with the children. I'm really so happy you can all be together, but my heart is breaking with longing for them. Please write me what the girls said when they saw you and what you, Moshko and you, Irma, said first. And how did they look to you? Does Helgichka go to school yet? She wanted to go to the Czech school next door to us — but she probably told you all that. I'm sure the little darlings have told you all about us here. Thank God, they are so bright, and it was so hard for me to be separated from them. Erwin and Elisha didn't want me to go to the train station with them, but Helgichka grabbed me and she said, "Grandma, I want to have you with me until the last minute," and Rayushka grabbed me by the hand too, and the trip to the train station was very hard. But, thank God, they are already there, safe and sound.

Here, everything is okay. Thank God Erwin now has work, so the time passes for him. I do the housework and to make the time go, I go to bed early and read many books so I don't have to think. Erwin goes out, because what is there to do at home? On Sundays I go to Papa at the cemetery. (I also visit Moshko's dear father there.) I spend some time there with him and go right home because where else is there to go? Now I see Faninka [Rabl] more often. This week he [Julius Rabl] will come home from the hospital. He often asks about the dear little girls and asks about you all. If they hadn't amputated his leg above the knee, he probably wouldn't be here — he had a very high fever, but is now doing well. He is really very good — so is Faninka. They were good to the girls, and are good to us. He got some "provisions" and gave us some. He will have to get used to the prosthesis.

Karl was with us, and would like to hear from you. Mother [Moshko's mother] comes every week and hopes we have a letter. She looks well — but we all have the same worries and troubles. Do you have enough companionship there? I don't. I'm not looking for any — I'm not very good at that. I'm glad when Erwin has some place to go — but I wait anxiously until he gets home.

So that's all for now. Please write soon and often and tell me everything. Maybe Helgichka can write to Rabl, he would really like that. Edith wrote to Aunt Rosa and sent pictures of Tomichek, and I saw them.

The Vogls are still in Radesovic; Brok is still employed, probably until January first; Hirschl is in Vienna; Paul Porges is in London and Franta Porges is here. [These are notes written in the margins of this letter.]

✉

Edith is one of Aunt Rosa Vogl's two daughters. Edith and Irma were the same age and shared many girlhood experiences — such as attending dancing school and taking Italian lessons from a private tutor. Edith became a musicologist, went to America in 1938 on business and prudently decided to remain there. Her brother Arnold, Aunt Rosa's only son, also emigrated to America at that early time. Edith struck up a strong friendship with Eleanor Roosevelt, which helped her to get her mother, Rosa, and her sister, Erna, into the United States. [See Appendix.]

"Hirschl" refers to *Franz Hirschl*, Aunt Clara's son, who at this time was living in Vienna, supposedly with a wealthy actress. He subsequently fled to the Soviet Union. When the Germans invaded Russia, Franz was sent to Siberia. He survived the war and died somewhere in the U.S.S.R.

Franta Porges, Uncle Rudolph's second son, was not deported until late in the war because his wife was Christian. He survived and is living in Prague with his wife Helena. (For Franta's brother Paul, see note to *Letter 22* above.)

Jews were officially barred from theatres and cinemas. The cost of attending these places of recreation was probably sufficiently prohibitive by this time.

[February, 1941.]

Museums, galleries and exhibitions were closed to Jews. All performances, public or recorded, of musical works involving Jews in any way, were prohibited; this included the distribution of sheet music.   [Late 1941.]

Letter 28
From Erwin

Masna Street 19
Prague
November 12, 1939

DEAR JOSEPH,

A few days ago I received your letter of October 15 in which you said you had received my two letters. Mainly, I wish you much luck on the opening of your office. It seems it will not be in Norwalk. I myself am somewhat busier than I have been for months, doing proctology especially, a field in which I have become known, so that other practitioners refer a number of cases to me. There is much belated news that a Jewish out-patient clinic has been established, with various departments — for instance: Neurology, headed by Prof. Sittig; for lung diseases, Hugo Adler; and I am in charge of my specialty. It won't be long until a Jewish hospital is opened. I have dropped for the moment my studies of languages, psychotherapy and other specialties since my professional activities take more of my time.

As you probably know, my nieces are happily reunited with their parents, which was a great worry. In spite of the fact that they created a problem in our apartment and in my practice, we had fun with them and we miss them very much. A number of my patients still ask me where the little assistants are: Helga cleaned the office, Raya took care of the waiting room — at a low salary. I hope that you saw them when they were in New York — if not, then you have missed a lot. I now have very few acquaintances in Prague. Most of them are "traveling." One doesn't have a great choice of destinations. My mother and I spend the evenings mostly reading. The libraries of all relatives — Rabl and acquaintances — are not big enough to satisfy one's needs. At present our projects have definitely "fallen in the water." The necessary documentation for State Board exams are resting on the bookshelf — forever?

I'm writing so dismally because this is a typewriter I'm not used to and the spaces between the keys feel strange.

Since not all letters arrive, I beg you to forward this letter to my sister.

WITH CORDIAL REGARDS TO YOU AND YOUR PARENTS,
ERWIN

[Appended to Erwin's letter]
DEAR HERR DOCTOR,

I thank you and your parents for your greetings and reciprocate them warmly with best wishes for your future. May God give you only happiness. I am very worried about my dear children, yet what can one do, one also has to accept one's fate, even though it is difficult.

YOURS,
PAULA

✉

Paula and Erwin appear to depend on the libraries of relatives for books. *Officially, in September 1941, all public libraries and lending libraries were declared off-limits to Jews.*

The sale of newspapers and other periodicals to Jews was prohibited. [May, 1942.]

Jews were required to surrender cameras, typewriters, adding machines, calculators, bicycles, portable musical instruments, furs, ski boots, skis and ski poles, and house pets: cats, dogs and birds. These could not be sold to Jews or given to them as gifts. [Summer, 1942.]

Erwin's reference to his "unfamiliar typewriter" could be a hint here that his usual machine was gone. After 1939 all of Erwin's letters were handwritten.

✉

Letter 29
From Erwin

Masna Street 19
Prague
November 29, 1939

DEAR JOSEPH,

Lately, we have received no mail from you or from my sister, so perhaps you have received none from us. Nevertheless, I am writing, and maybe one or the other of the letters will arrive — and if this letter should arrive, please forward it to St. Louis to the Shell Building.

The main thing is, my mother and I are well. Lately, I have been earning a satisfactory living.

Recently again, people in my profession have been able to emigrate if they have a visa for a neutral country. As for the USA, the situation is not good because my waiting time would be about one and one-half years if not longer. The other countries, like Uruguay etc., charge so much for landing — money that it's impossible to afford with our currency. The cheapest thing is to wait — so that's all I can do.

During the day I have enough work at home, and afterwards some house calls. In the evening I am often invited to go somewhere, but I go to the coffee-house very rarely — which has its reasons. About eleven o'clock I come home where my mother is usually waiting up for me worriedly — that means, she is in bed reading some borrowed book or other.

Since I can only write you unimportant things, I will close this letter and just send greetings to you, your parents — and perhaps, if you forward this letter, to my sister, my brother-in-law and my dear nieces.

ERWIN

[P.S.] Almost daily, a friend or loyal patient who is emigrating comes to say goodbye. Most go to Palestine. How goes gastroscopy in the USA?

Erwin can write only "unimportant things" because of the Nazi censorship. He goes rarely to the coffee-house because Jews were increasingly barred from public places.

Letter 30   Masna Street 19
From Paula   Prague
                                               December, 1939

MY DEAREST CHILDREN AND LITTLE ONES:

   I'm writing because Karl is to take this letter and he is
supposed to leave tomorrow but they did not come to visit me
— even so, I think they are at the Poppers and if they are, that is
nearby. We are sending this letter to Karl via your dear mother,
and we are waiting anxiously for a few words from you. We
wrote a few times, but I don't know whether you received them.
I hope something arrived. I'm lonesome for you, and I hope I
will see you again and we can all be together. Often, I can't
believe it's true that you're so far away. If I could at least have
a letter from you then I might believe it. Aunt Rosa does get
letters, and asks whether we get any, and we don't. Do you have
an apartment? Every day I wait for the mailman.

   I hope, Shishinko, that you are well, the children and
the household give you a lot to do but I beg you to take the
time and write at least two lines so I can again see your
handwriting. You can't imagine how I miss you here. I think
of you all the time, and it calms me to know you are in freedom
and safety. I would be so happy if Erwin were safe. If that were
so, I could patiently tolerate everything. You, dear Moshko, have
a good job, the same as here? If you would take the pen in your
hand and write me all about you, how you are getting along there,
whether you are well, how your apartment is furnished, how the
weather is, how the children are! Does dear Helga go to school?
Do they learn and speak English? Do they remember us and
think of us? Oh, I have so many questions but you don't have
time to write a long letter and I can only wish for it and wait. I

am sending a little sweater for the children with Karl, I just finished knitting it, but you have to do something with the arms because I had to use a different yarn but you will have to unravel it. I didn't have time to finish it because Karl is leaving. I hope it passes customs. It is very hard to get yarn and one has to take what there is. That's how it is with everything. Thank God the dear children were able to leave in time — but my heart went with them. But it is better that you are there. Here, things go on and the important thing is we mustn't lose hope and we must trust in God. Only, please write, even if only once a month if you can't do it more often and in your letter tell me everything about yourselves and the children.

> I greet and kiss you all,
> YOUR LONESOME MOTHER

MY DEAR LITTLE ONES:

What are you doing all the time, and how are you? Helga should write me, with Raya, a long letter — Rabl always asks whether you still remember him. If only we could all hug each other, as we always used to do, when we played together with him. Does Tommy walk and talk? And how do you like school, Helga? My Rayushko, are you good? I love you very much and am lonesome for you. I kiss all of you.

> YOUR BABICHKA

If God wills it, then maybe we will see each other again after all.

✉

Karl, Max's brother, was about to emigrate. The Poppers were Karl's non-Jewish in-laws. It was possible that Paula wished Karl to deliver the letter when he reached the US, because the post office on Ostrovni Street was very far from Masna Street.

All post offices in Greater Prague were off-limits to Jews, except the one on Ostrovni Street, which was open to Jews only between the hours of one and three in the afternoon. [September, 1941.]

Letter 31   Masna Street 19
From Erwin   Prague
                                              December 3, 1939
DEAR IMSCHA AND MOSHKO,

Since I must finish this letter quickly because Karl is taking it along, I won't "schmooze" very much but will remain very factual. Recently, it has begun to look once more as though I might emigrate, not only might, but perhaps should or even must. Because of this, I must ask you to undertake something which is not possible from here. The United States is out of the question because the wait for a visa would be two years or longer so that would be wasted effort. Another neutral country, Sweden? Chile? etc. I am sending you the translated *curriculum vitae* as you requested. Send it to whomever you trust: Sperling, Fleischmann, Boros, etc. Now it is really urgent.

Now that I am working again and no longer have the expense of the children and Elisha, I can afford to give the 3000 Kr. to your mother [Max's mother]. I felt embarrassed that I couldn't give it to her until now but she never asked for it directly — and does not even now. The first of June I received 5000 Kr. and then, again, 5000 Kr. from you, and I got 3000 Kr. for the kitchen and 375 for the sofa and then again 3000 for your mother. For the children I spent (as I already told you in detail) 2080 Kr.. I told you before that I had 7,400 Kr. left but I actually have 10,434 Kr. Dr Katz asked that you pay 1895 Kr. which he claims you owed him. I promised him I would tell you about it. Your tax for the Jewish Community has not been paid! Because of the housecleaning, we did not have to pay it. I am sure you know from Elisha that I got nothing from Uncle Rudolph, so you need subtract nothing from the 10,343 Kr.

mentioned above. I hope that Paul [Porges] didn't get anything out of Armin either — otherwise he would have to pay it back.

Sperling has photostats of all of my medical documents. Only two are missing and I enclose them now. I got them through Dr Gutheil even though he doesn't know me; he wanted to try to help me somehow. I received that transcript at the beginning of September.

Write soon. Mama yearns for a letter from you. Other people seem to be getting mail more often from their relatives in the USA.

With best regards and kisses, to all of you and the dear children.

ERWIN

December 3, 1939

[DEAR HELGICHKA AND RAYUSHKA,]

You will now know English better than your uncle "Ewinek" but your uncle can still kick the ball off the back of the sofa so that it hits the ceiling much better than you! Mrs Cohen sends greetings and Rablichek asked whether you have written to your grandmother — who, like your uncle, thinks of you very often. Be well, eat a lot, and stay good little girls.

A MILLION KISSES FROM YOUR
UNCLE ERWIN

✉

Erwin's comment that he "might, should or perhaps must," emigrate is a reference to the fact that Jews were periodically forced to emigrate in 1939. For varying periods they were given the choice of finding a country to accept them immediately (all but impossible in most cases), or being sent to concentration camps like Dachau in Germany.

The Jewish Community to which Erwin refers was, before the Occupation, a vestige of the days when Jews were not assimilated into Czech life. Most Prague Jews paid fees to the Community out of habit, and turned to it only at times of birth, death and often marriage. The Community services, which concentrated on religious observances and small charities, were housed in the old Jewish municipality building. But when the Nazis cut off Jews from the life of the country, the Jewish Community became much more important. The taxes helped to pay for courses in new skills and in foreign languages (mostly English and Spanish) — in eternal preparation for emigration. The Jewish Community — which, as time went on, worked closely with Zionist organizations — became the only central Jewish leadership.

Erwin's reference to the "housecleaning" is not clear.

✉

Letter 32   Masna Street 19
From Paula   Prague
                                                December 29, 1939

MY DEAREST CHILDREN,

How often I've written you already! Letters and cards, because I think something will reach you, and I wait impatiently for the postman because I think that some day there has to be a letter from you. And so, I wait and wait.

Karl must certainly be there [in the U.S.] already. Is he going to come to you? We couldn't discuss anything with him when he came here because he was in a great hurry — and we would have liked to discuss a few things with him that we wanted him to tell you. We gave him a letter and several of Erwin's documents to take along; and I'm sure you got them already. Today Mr Pick, Hella's father, was here and he brought us a letter from Elisha. Your dear mother, Moshko, had told us everything in it. I already knew what the letter said, but I enjoyed it anyway. Hella wrote how exciting it was when you, Moshko, greeted the children, how you all wept with joy. I can clearly visualize it. And you, dear Shishinko! I'm already so lonesome for all of you. I've wept oceans of tears for you and the little ones. It was so lively here with them. I have to look at their pictures all the time. In my mind, they are still around me. I'm so sad, and I hope I'll awaken from this grief and we will all meet. If only it could be soon! I wonder whether my darling girls remember all about us and tell you about us. I repeat to myself what they used to say and I see them in front of me and I hug them! I'm sure Helgichka is already in school, and Rayushka . . . if only I could squeeze them! And you, the grown-up children with them!

We are well. Erwin has work to do and I pass the time here and there. I don't even know how the day passes. It is short, it is evening quickly, I crawl into my bed and read and think of you and pray for you. I would love to know how you manage. Do you have a maid, or somebody for the children? What kind of apartment do you have? I would like to hear about everything! Now I think we will get a letter from you. Please write very soon. About Uncle Rabl: I don't know if you know his leg was amputated. I wrote you about it. Erwin Rabl married a girl from here — she went to join him. The elderly Mrs Koretz died. Aninka Schnurmacher is going to have a baby! Arnold went to Italy last week, and many friends have left. Dr Wolff Guttman went to Palestine. Aunt Rosa receives a letter from Edith every two or three weeks, and I ask myself, why none from you?

Aninka Schnurmacher is Aunt Malva's daughter, married to Franta Brezak, a Gentile. The child she was expecting — Marie — was born in 1940. A son, Franta , was born in 1942. All of them survived. Aninka still lives in a house in Czechoslovakia which has been in her family for 400 years.

[P.S.] MY DARLING LITTLE GIRLS,

Now you are with your parents and Tomichek again and I don't have you here and I'm very lonesome for you. I wonder whether you still remember us! Where is the long letter, darling Helgichka? I would like to hug you the way I used to. And you, my Rayushka: the games we played together! I see your little eyes in front of me, and in the evening I think I have Helgichka in my bed with me. My darling little dumplings, I hug all three of you. Stay well all of you, I kiss you all, and Helgichka, write us – after all, you know how, and Rayushka does too!

GOODBYE MY DARLINGS AND STAY WELL.

GRANDMA

[Note in margin:] Your mother, Lotte and Ettel are well taken care of. Many kisses,

ERWIN

Letter 33   Masna Street 19
From Paula   Prague
                                       January 1, 1940
MY DEAREST, DARLING CHILDREN,

 On the last day of the old year I received your card that was written on October 23rd. In that card you tell me you are expecting the children — that you, dear Irma, are at home in St. Louis and Max is in New York. The telegram arrived and as you see, the card came yesterday. Did you get any of our letters? We are happy that, at long last, we heard from you. You wrote that you got practical presents for your birthday — that's what Moshko *should* get you now. The important thing is that you use them in happiness and health. Now it will soon be Moshko's birthday, so I want to congratulate you on behalf of "the Praguers." Dear Tomichek must be running by now, as he already started walking two months ago. If I could only see all of you! It is useless for us to send you pictures, because we don't know if you would get them. We are well, thank God, and we are delighted that you are too. Moshko, your mother is also well and she looks very well. Did Elisha give you the money? Your mother came to see us, and one of these days I will go there.

YOUR MAMA

My darling little children: I send you many kisses.

YOUR BABICHKA

P.S. January 2, 1940

I am so happy, today I received a letter from you, with some words from my darling little sweethearts. I promise you a long letter. It is very cold here, today there is snow. Again, love and kisses.

January 2, 1940

Just now we received the letter that was mailed in October from New York. You described the apartment — the children will love the yard. We are quite well; I have been working very little since March 1939. As I already wrote you, I took over my specialty in the Jewish Community ambulatory clinic, but without pay. I sent photostats of my papers on gastroscopy and my diplomas to Sperling.

MANY KISSES,
ERWIN

Letter 34   Masna Street 19
From Erwin   Prague
                                                     January, 1940
DEAR MOSHKO AND IMSHKO,

Thank you for your dear letter of January 2, and now it
is finally possible for Mother and me to get visas from you —
but what we need is for you to buy boat tickets and also for your
dear mother whom we want to bring with us. We hope and pray
so much that our dreams will come true with your help. We are
writing to the American consulate in Vienna for our visas, and
we hope that Mother's affidavit from you and mine from Mrs
Schanzer will be okay. We must then go via Vienna. We hope
that you can get the boat ticket and visas. The visas depend on
our having a boat ticket. If it should be necessary to go to see
Mrs Schanzer, maybe Joseph Sperling can do it; I am writing
to him today after a long interval. Be well. The photos of you
and the children are beautiful and each grandmother has one.
We thank you in advance and send heartfelt greetings from

ERWIN

*In January of 1940, Jewish bank accounts
were officially frozen. Transfers of savings
accounts and securities required the con-
sent of the Treasury Department, to which
Jews had to apply for a special permit in
order to withdraw more than 1,500 Kr.
[approximately $60] per week from their
accounts for themselves and their families.*

Letter 35 Masna Street 19
From Paula Prague
March 24, 1940

MY DEAREST, BELOVED, GOLDEN CHILDREN AND LITTLE ONES:

Now, thank God, I have received some letters from you — and a postcard dated November 18th and a letter from November 20th. Also from the 27th of November and the 16th of December. I have no words to tell you the pleasure I get from your letters, and that I can read about you. And I will answer all of them at the same time. In the evenings I read and re-read the letters in bed and by now I know them by heart. It is as if I hear your voices. You, dear Rayusko, should keep your coat on! You, dear Helgaleh, are so reasonable — and our little tiny one, he sleeps? And you, my dear grown-ups are, thank God, well. I see you all in front of me and I would like to kiss all of you.

And now I want to answer all your questions: So we also wrote several letters and a card every week. Maybe you will get them. I sent a letter with Dr Milder, did you get it? I tried to send you some embroidered goods with Karl — but thank God the children have enough to wear. I had to make it because there is nothing to be bought any more. That the little ones already speak good English doesn't surprise me at all. They are very well-endowed intellectually. But I'm very happy about it and quite proud of it because I had something to do with it. Everyone liked them very much, and we miss them. Even in the street people stopped to look at them. They even ask about the littlest one, dear Tomichek. Perhaps God may will it that we may see each other again and be together. You had to endure missing your children, just as I do.

It's very hard for me to describe my feelings. I would like to be everywhere. You will understand me if I tell you, dear Shishinko, how you have so much work, I would like to fly there and help you — I would like to at least visit. With God's help everything will turn out well and I'm thanking the Almighty that you are there and that you are well. Thank God I am well and you should always be happy and so too should Erwin and I. It is so difficult to be away from you. If you cut your hand, you miss your finger. So I will leave it up to God, whatever He wants to do. I am sure by now you have somebody to help you because it's too much for you — Moshko has enough to do with his work, he won't be able to help you in the house. Besides, he doesn't know how. I know that the girls can pretty much take care of themselves but they still require a bit of work and I know you always want everything in good order. In my mind I worry that if you do too much when you're young, you'll feel it when you're old. But maybe work is good for you — but not too much. But you know that yourself — as time passes you find that out. You have to have someone to help you — how is it with the Negroes? I hear they are supposed to be very hard-working and very reliable. Can they cook too? I'm very happy that you can cook well, dear Shishinko, and I hope that Moshko likes your cooking. I want you to let me know that that's true, because I know my darling daughter! Uncle Alois is no longer working.

My darling, golden Helgichka: I am so happy to hear that you are doing so well in school. Do you remember how you told me we would walk and talk together? If that could only happen! I always remember and think of you so I know your ears must be ringing: you, my darling exceptional girl! Why are you so far away? I hope we will be together soon. In my mind I hug you the way I always did in bed. Rabl often talks of you, you should write him when you have time. Erwin too is very happy with your letters. Did you stop fighting with Raya? That's not nice, fighting. I kiss you my darling, and be good and happy.

GREETINGS FROM YOUR
BABICHKA

P.S. Do you remember your uncle telling you stories?

✉

An edict was issued that Jews could not receive ration cards for clothing, but must buy clothes from old clothes dealers. They were prohibited specifically from buying new caps, suitcases, knapsacks, briefcases, shopping and other bags, purses and leather straps.

Although this edict was not formalized until October 1940, it was surely in force even six months before this letter ("there is nothing to be bought any more"). Helga and Raya recall that just prior to their leaving Prague, Paula sent them outside to soil and scuff new shoes she had bought them for the journey, to make them look old and worn to the officials. The girls thought it was hilarious to be told the opposite of what they had been so carefully taught about new shoes, and remember still how difficult it was to dirty the white stitching.

Uncle Alois was "no longer working" because his gift shop on Wenceslaus Square had been "Aryanized" — that is, confiscated. "Trustees" were appointed to run good-sized Jewish businesses; the owners were dismissed.

✉

The Froehlich Family: {l to r} Erwin, Leopold, Paula and Irma circa 1910.

Paula Froehlich circa 1939.

Erwin on hospital
rounds circa 1935.

Erwin {rear, second from right} and colleagues circa 1935.

Max and Irma skiing in Tatras Mountains circa 1931.

Irma at her easel in Prague Park, 1925.

Paula and Irma on a Prague street, circa 1935.

Newspaper clipping describing luxury building
in which Czerners lived at the time of the Occupation:
"A garage even for baby-buggies".

Garage selbst für Kinderwagen

Prag. In dem soeben erschienenen ersten Heft der neuen interessanten Zeitschrift „Architektura Č. S. R." wird ein neues großes Wohnhaus gezeigt, welches in Prag-Dejwitz, Dürichplatz, vom Architekten K. F. Podzemný erbaut wurde. Es ist eines der größ-

Chauffeure aufgebaut. Anschließend an diese Garage befindet sich ein geräumer Luftschutzkeller und darüber ein Tennisplatz für die Bewohner des Hauses. Das Erdgeschoß enthält zu beiden Seiten des Haupteingangs sieben Geschäftslokale, so daß der

ten Prager Wohnblocks, der in seiner Anlage mit allen Errungenschaften der modernen Bautechnik ausgestattet ist. Etwa 60 Wohnungen befinden sich hier und sind bereits durchwegs vermietet. Bauherr dieses mächtigen Hauses ist die Landesbank. Die einzelnen Wohnungen sind typisiert und unterscheiden sich untereinander nur durch die Zimmeranzahl. Alle Räume samt Zubehör werden direkt ohne Luftschacht belichtet und gelüftet. Geheizt wird der Bau durch eine moderne Deckenheizung, deren Kesselraum mit Zentralregulierung im zweiten Kellergeschoß untergebracht ist. Im Keller befindet sich auch eine riesige Zentral-Waschküche für alle Parteien. In dem Garten, der vom Stiegenhaus zugänglich ist, wurde eine Garage mit einer dazugehörigen Reparaturwerkstätte und mit Aufenthaltsräumen für

Neubau auch eine geschäftliche Belebung dieses Stadtviertels mit sich bringt. In den einzelnen Stockwerken sind je zwei Wohnungen, wobei die Vierzimmerwohnungen neben einer Terrasse auch einen Wintergarten haben. Eine große Dachterrasse soll die Freizeit der Bewohner verschönern. Hier, auf diesem geräumigen Dachgarten, sind zum Teil gedeckte Liegeplätze, Sandbecken für Kinder, Blumenbeete und Duschen. Der Zins bewegt sich zwischen 11.000 und 19.000 K. Der Bauherr hat mit Familien gerechnet, die auch Kinder haben und so hat das Haus auch eine kleine Garage für Kinderwagen. In Reih und Glied kann man hier am frühen Nachmittag die Kinderwagen ausfahren sehen. Unser Bild zeigt den großen Block, in dem heute bereits fast 300 Menschen leben.

Irma with Raya, Helga with Max in Prague, 1938.

The Czerners with new baby – Tomicek – Prague, 1939.

On deck of the Rotterdam: Elisha top row far left. Helga and Raya in light gray coats; Hella on chair far right. Others are unidentified.

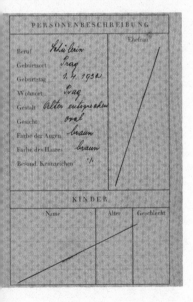

On Helga's passport, as on the passports of all Jewish females, the middle name "Sara" was inserted. Jewish males were given the middle name of "Israel".

Raya's passport is stamped with a large "J" as were those of all Jews.

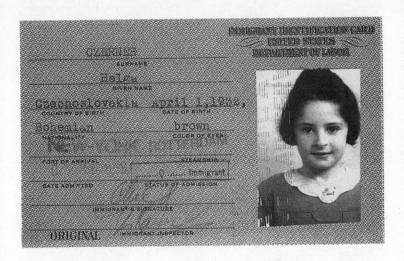

Helga's "green card".

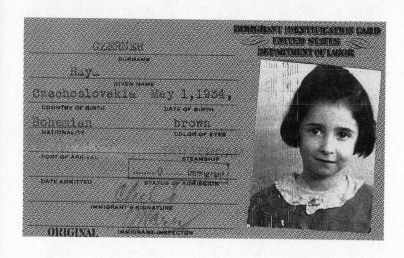

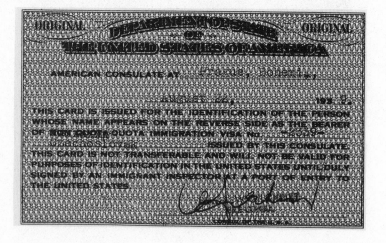

Raya's "green card".

19 Masna Street.
The Froehlichs had the first floor appartment.

(1989 photograph)

Letter 36 Masna Street 19
From Erwin Prague
April, 1940

DEAR IRMA AND MOSHKO,

Since Mother has written so much, I'll add only a little. We have to change our residence — do not know yet where to, since apartments are hard to get. To answer your question, I don't charge for my services in my practice. All the advice from you and Armin is not practical; and I have to wait about five years in order to come to the USA. This was the situation when Karl was still here and nothing has changed. More soon — cordial kisses,

ERWIN

Moving into smaller and smaller apartments was forced upon Jews by the Nazis. *Jews could no longer rent vacant apartments; they were forced to move into apartments already occupied by other Jews. When their leases expired, they could be renewed only with the permission of the* Zentralstelle. *There was no legal protection for Jews against termination of their leases. And, unlike apartments leased by non-Jewish tenants, apartments occupied by Jews were not rent-controlled. [September 13, 1940.]*

From Paula

Your dear mother, Moshko, is here now and since she doesn't want to write in Hebrew, she asked if I would write this for her:

I was at the consulate and he said that there was $1500 deposited and that this is too little, and he advises that you and Elisha should vouch for the amount that you could provide her [Mother Czerner] monthly and that you should send her affidavit. As for Lotte, she might be able to get out, but only after four years. You, Moshko, should arrange that Lotte perhaps travel with her as a 'companion,' and could maybe live with your mother there in an apartment, as your mother's caretaker. Ettel can look out for herself.

This is the dictation that your dear mother gave me and she sends her greetings to all of you. Do write me again soon. It is a pity that there is such a long time between letters and that they arrive so slowly and irregularly. Again, many greetings and I kiss you all a thousand times.

Your Mama

✉

As noted above, Paula confused Hebrew and Yiddish; Mother Czerner could write some Yiddish, apparently, but not Hebrew. Although Paula says Mother Czerner "dictated" the letter, Paula has written it referring to Mother Czerner in the third person.

✉

To *Prague*

Letter 37   808A Pennsylvania Avenue
From Irma   University City, Missouri
                                                           April 6, 1940

MY DEAREST MOTHER AND BROTHER,

We greatly enjoyed your letter of February 12 in which you answered our joint card of November 6. It's interesting that about two weeks before it arrived, your card of February 19th came — but we are happy to get news of you and we hope to get more soon. Until, with God's help, we see each other again. I would be so happy to be with you!

Here it is a beautiful spring. I am on the balcony with Tomichek — he sleeps while I cook. It's Friday and so I'm cooking for the whole weekend. Dear Moshko is very hardworking — he works, and in the evening he studies English and helps me in the house whenever he can. I am not lazy myself and I am happy that, thank God, we are all well. Often in my mind I am with you, Maminko, and I ask for your advice. And I hope something rubbed off on me. Often I find out that in practical matters you and Moshko are alike — and often, when we joke, I think I am talking to you!

Helgichka had a nice birthday — she is, knock on wood, a young lady. They got "roller skates" for their birthday — those are ice-skates with wheels, all the kids have them and fly around on them; she also got summer clothes, socks, and a bed for a doll from Raya. Thank God we are making a combined birthday party for both of them. This is almost a cult here, what one does for the children! Our girls speak English already "a mile a minute." Only Raya sometimes mixes English and Czech but she doesn't care, she says Grandma used to say "*Snupak* is English for *Kapesnik*." [In Czech both "*snupak*" and "*kapesnik*" mean "handkerchief."] Now that it's nice weather I hardly see them all day. Helga goes to school in the morning and has lunch there and comes home about 3:30 with Raya, who goes to kindergarten at noon. Before that she plays outside the house until lunch. They come home and drink their milk and play outside again. The walk to school is a nice one and around our house there are trees and grass – so going for "walks" is not necessary. Only Tomichek dances around me and, thank God, he's almost two. Most people say he looks like Moshko, but his eyes are dark like mine. He is a darling, lively boy – his eyes dart around and he likes to smile and show his pretty teeth. We call him "Tomichek" and he blows kisses, which is delightful. What he likes best is to clean up. He carries books and gives them to me – or toys and dishes. And then I must put everything back. We don't go out much – only occasionally somebody takes us out in his car or we are invited somewhere.

What are the Slonitzes doing, and all the relatives and people we know? Did you get our November letter with the picture in the park? And the postcard-type photo? We sent them to you and to Bulharska [Street]. Did they [Moshko's family] get our letters, and did they write us something? Stay well all of you and write us – from Masna and from Bulharska – a lot and soon!

Letter 38 Masna Street 19
From Paula Prague
April 7, 1940

MY DEAREST CHILDREN,

Just now I received a letter written March 10th. I called to tell Mrs Wolff that there were greetings for her, I called her right away because she would be so happy, but she wasn't home. I gave her the greetings the next morning, and she had a letter from you. I told your mother about it right away, Moshko, and she came and read everything. The pictures weren't there, only the one you sent for your mother was there, and that one she now has. My darling, darling children, as long as I know you're all well! I live in the hope that God will bring us all together; this hope, and prayer, make us strong. I know you have received nothing from us, although I wrote you a long and newsy letter, and also a card. Maybe the mail takes a long time and they're still en route.

Are the girls getting used to the Negro woman? Do you understand her? Is she any help to you? I can imagine that you have less work now that the sweet girls are in school and there's also some relief since Moshko doesn't come home for lunch.

If I could only just look at you, and be with you *all* for just a little while! Did you need to buy any furniture? Sleeping is better in a bed, no? I'm surprised, Moshko, that you still need to study English — after all, you know it so well! But you are never satisfied with yourself. That doesn't hurt. As long as others are satisfied with you.

I'm surprised that Helgaleh has been accepted into the second grade. I thought she would have to repeat. But, after all, she is my golden girl. I have a notebook of hers that I saved because her hands touched it and she wrote it in pencil. This notebook I kiss all the time and I take it with me wherever I go. And my Rayushka probably speaks English very well, and I can't, so I'll let her speak for me.

We move on April 12. We will be in Pariska Street (Nurembergstrasse), 32. It is a four-room apartment. It is an old building and it will be hard to get used to, but what can you do? It will work out somehow. In summer it will be all right, but we don't know how it will be in winter. I already wrote you that everyone in this building has to move. Otherwise, thank God, we are well and Erwin now has, thank God, enough work. Mother Czerner does not want to leave now. She would only leave if Tante Steffi made it necessary, because under no circumstance does she want to leave Lotte and Ettel. If she emigrates and then Tante Steffi is kicked out, what will she do over there?

MUCH, MUCH LOVE,

MAMA

✉

Paula says that she cannot speak English, but in the early days of the Occupation, when there was still money and hope, she took English lessons and was doing quite well.

✉

[P.S.] My darling little children: I got so much pleasure from your letter! How famous my Helgichka is, and how my Rayulichka already speaks English so well to everybody. I tell everyone about my wonderful kids in America, and even Tomichek already knows how to dance and sing. How I would love to see you play and to hug you. And how is it there? Do you have weiners and little sandwiches and everything you like to eat? Now summer is coming, and I will remember again how we rode to Zbraslav. Stay well, I kiss and greet you all.

April 8-9, 1940: "Blitzkrieg": Germany invaded Denmark and Norway. Denmark did not resist. Norway was defeated by June 10th.

Letter 39
From Mother Czerner
[Prague
April or May, 1940]

MY DEAR CHILDREN,

Be well and happy; your mother greets you and prays we will soon see each other. I have all the documents in order but I don't want to leave without Lotte. Maybe with some bribes you could arrange things. See if you can take care of the boat ticket there, since now we do not know which boat we could go on.

KISSES,
MOTHER
Also for the children.

P.S. So that you know where we are, Pariska Street is now Nurembergstrasse.

✉

> This brief note from Max's mother (written on a scrap of paper) was actually written by Paula, who added a postscript about the Pariska Street address which was, of course, Paula's and Erwin's address — not the Czerners'. Mother Czerner, Ettel and Lotte remained in Bulharska Street.
>
> Many Prague street names, especially those offensive to the Nazi regime, such as "Paris Street" (Pariska), were changed overnight. ✉

Letter 40
From Paula

Nurembergstrasse 32
Prague
May, 1940

MY DEAR, DEAR, BELOVED CHILDREN:

I love your little letter — you wrote so prettily and I was very happy with it. Did Tomichek break any dishes when he helped you dry them? He is quite a little worker and you must have great fun with him. I see you all the time in front of me and your dear picture I have next to me all the time and show it to everyone. You, my darling Helgichka, are quite grown up, already in the second grade, and I congratulate you on your success. After all, I know my Rayushinka is a hard worker. You know, my darling girls, how I would love to fly to you the way I could when you were in Dejvice, but unfortunately now it's much farther away; but I don't lose hope that God will eventually make it possible — but in my thoughts I hug you. And then we'll send your parents out dancing and I will watch you and tell you stories, but not in English because I would make such a hash of it with my bad English that you wouldn't even understand them! You, my dear Raya, probably also speak good English with Helga and probably also with Tomichek and probably also draw very nicely, even better than I. I know you are glad to be with your parents and we are so happy that things are good for you — that you have good people there and the nicest friends. I am your friend too, but far away — but you are also my dearest ones. Give each other lots of kisses for me — also your Daddy and Mommy and Tommy. Such good kisses that I can hear the smack all the way to Prague! And be good and happy and merry. I kiss you with 1,000,000,000,000,000 kisses, you can't even count them, my darlings!

YOUR LOVING GRANDMA

(Your Grandma Czerner also wishes to greet and kiss you.)

Dejvice was the location of Irma and
Max's last apartment in Prague.

Letter 41
From Erwin

Nurembergstrasse 32
Prague
May, 1940

DEAR IRMA AND MOSHKO:

One after another, two letters came from you and today one from Sperling. (The Sperling letter was dated April 14, 1940.) I thank you for my birthday wishes. On my birthday I received congratulations from Tante Steffi, and this was very expensive. This was just at the time that we had to move. You keep writing about Bolivia, but it is totally impossible to get the visa; in spite of the fact that it would be very good, it's not possible for me. One thing that other people make use of when they wish to emigrate and can be supported by relatives is to go to Shanghai. I have a lot of work, but unfortunately it won't last much longer.

SINCERELY,
ERWIN

MY HELGICHKA AND RAYUSKO!

When we come to America, we will go together and have a look at your pretty school — if you take me along, that is. Did you write to everyone in your little address book? And do you still remember what it looks like here? But where you are it's probably much prettier. Rablichek was very happy to get regards from you.

HEARTFELT KISSES,
YOUR UNCLE ERWIN

Letter 42
From Julius Rabl   Zbraslav
To Irma and Max   May 7, 1940

DEAR FRIENDS,

I received your letter of January 26th. This is the first letter I've had from you and we were very happy with the contents, and the main thing, that you are well. Here, everyone is well and content. Except for my leg, I consider my status satisfactory. I can understand how you were pining for your children in the beginning, but there was nothing you could do about it. Parents are more important for children than grandmother and uncle. They [the children] will keep forever their memories of days here with us swimming in the river and picking fruit from the trees — we had all day to enjoy nature. The poet Jablonsky says that for the doer, a good deed is preserved in the petals of a flower; but for the recipient, it is preserved in marble. Horace says: *Multis illa bonis flebilis* [sic] *occidit.*

You are across the ocean in a free country, and you are not excessively dependent on the kindness of others. And for this we praise God and thank Him for His effort on behalf of your parents. Man is dependent on God, and it is good to have friendly relations with those around us. "Good" means not doing evil. God can live only in a satisfied and happy heart, and that you can achieve. Character is more valuable than intelligence, and therefore I think we have enough wisdom and ability to withstand deprivation. Our parents were happier than we, and had less. Endurance is more important than genius.

The daily thought of death impels me to marshal my

strength, to thank life for its gifts and to recognize and accept fate. Stay well and be assured of our love.

JULIUS AND FANNY

DEAREST CHILDREN,

Thank you for your letter. I liked your descriptions. Don't make your parents angry, and be grateful that they gave you life. I loved you a lot. When you sometimes made me angry I gladly forgave you. Don't forget your precious homeland, and be good and observant Jews and God will protect you. Amen.

WITH KISSES,
YOUR RABLICHEK AND AUNT FANNY

✉

Julius Rabl, like many Czech Jews, was strongly patriotic. It has been documented that Czech Jews went into the gas chambers singing the Czech national anthem. And Raya was told that Rabl himself sang the Czech anthem when he was deported. Another reflection of this patriotism is the fact that Max Czerner, a deeply religious man, named his son after Thomas Masaryk, the first president of Czechoslovakia, despite the fact that in Jewish families it is customary to name children after deceased family members.

In May, 1940, the Germans invaded and conquered Luxembourg, Holland, Belgium and France, and moved rapidly to the English Channel. The Allies were evacuated from the continent at Dunkirk. Italy entered the war on Germany's side on June 10.

✉

Letter 43
From Erwin

Nurembergstrasse 32
Prague
June 25, 1940

DEAR IRMA AND MOSHKO:

I sent your affidavit to the consulate, but the quota will still be closed for several years and then it will be four years before the visa comes. I have to find Dr Katz's address. We are quite well. Next month it will be decided whether I can go on working. Your [Moshko's] mother, as far as her health is concerned, is fine.

GREETINGS,
ERWIN

DEAREST CHILDREN,

I send you many kisses.

YOUR UNCLE.

P.S. I found out that Franz Hirschl married a very nice girl — he was engaged to her. That's how the Hirschls got out.

Mother is, thank God, healthy. This week she had an examination because she gets cold easily but the main thing is she is healthy.

Children: enjoy your vacation in good health!

✉

There seems to be some confusion about Franz Hirschl, who was in Vienna in November of 1939 [See *Letter 27n*]. The Hirschls mentioned here must be Franz and his wife, because his parents did not survive. This marriage evidently enabled Franz to emigrate to Russia.

Letter 44   Nurembergstrasse 32
From Paula   Prague
                                           August, 1940

[DEAR CHILDREN,]

Again you will have lots of work with the moving, and I can't help you. If only you were all together with everything in order — but September is not so far away. I wrote you about the numbering but I do not even remember myself how to figure it. I don't have the head for it, I'm so confused. Now you are already used to your new country and with God's help you will adjust to the new city. Like [Edith] Slonitz, I try to keep up with all the acquaintances. Do you, my darling Shishinko, want to know how we look? Everyone says both of us look well.

Maybe the work is good for me and I wonder myself how God gives us the strength. I go shopping at eleven o'clock — and what I can't manage to get, I have to go at three o'clock or the next day. This way I have something to do morning and afternoon — and I don't even consider just going for a walk because all of the benches are occupied and one does not even have a place to sit down. We were all in Pilsen at Aunt Clara's and I already wrote you about Uncle Schanzer. Yesterday I was in Zbraslav. I go there every Sunday with dear Erwin, even for a whole day. At eight o'clock we are home. Dear Erwin is home every night and he studies — from one book in German and the same book in English. These are the same books. I get tired and go to sleep with a prayer and thinking of you I sleep until morning. In Zbraslav I see my darling girls in front of me as they were last year and I am so happy that they are better off now. I phoned Babichka [Grandmother] Czerner that I got a letter, so tomorrow she'll come here and I'll let her read it. Mrs Fleischmann came to see us and she wanted to know if you have any news about Franta. I said I would ask you. What do you think, Shishinko, of the fact that we made a tablecloth from your little doilies because ours was torn — and everybody loves it! Now I really have a lot of work, because I must get all my belongings into two rooms or maybe I'll put some in the bathroom because there is an order that we must "rent" out two rooms. At least I won't have to clean there! Also, I don't have bedspreads or comforters or closets. I hope it is rented soon, because the rooms are large and clean. This letter I will give to the Slonitzes. I'll bet you were happy that Edith came to you and now you can get together with Hedy. So be well. I kiss you all 100,000 times and love you forever.

MAMINKA

✉

Irma and Max were moving from St Louis to Chicago in September because Max's employment with Shell was terminated. Edith Vogl came to St Louis to help with the move. She looked after the children while Max and Irma hunted for an apartment.

Paula's reference to "numbering" may have something to do with preparations for Irma's move.

Paula had to go shopping for food at eleven a.m. and three p.m. because these were the only hours Jews were allowed to shop. There were consequently long lines and restricted availability of food.

Jews could no longer receive ration cards for apples; vegetables; special rations of sugar; tobacco products; jellies and preserves; shaving soap; special soap rations for children over the age of one year; all fruits – fresh, dried and canned; nuts; cheese; candies; fish and fish products; poultry; venison; carp; wine and liquor; onions, garlic and pork. In addition, they could not be given fishing licenses or consumer identification cards for unrationed provisions. [October, 1940.] Before the end of 1942 the list of prohibited foods was enlarged to include all meats, eggs, rolls, cakes, white bread and milk (children under six could receive milk), honey and yeast.

Laws were handed down by the police that Jews were forbidden to enter certain streets in the vicinity of the Produce Exchange on days when the Exchange was open for business. [December, 1940.]

Paula could not sit down on public benches because this was prohibited to Jews. *Public parks and gardens in Prague were declared off–limits to Jews. [May, 1940.]*

Paula and Erwin were home at eight o'clock at night because of the curfew.

Mrs Ella Fleischmann, also referred to in the letters as "Frau Fleischmann," was the mother of Franta Fleischmann (See *Letter 17n*). Franta or Franz, as mentioned previously, escaped to England with his wife, also named Ella, and daughter Eva [Evichka], a playmate of Helga and Raya's. The three returned to Czechoslovakia after the war where Franta rose in the ranks of the government. Mrs Fleischmann [the grandmother] did not survive.

Segregated Jewish areas in restaurants and other public places were discontinued. Jews could not use them at all. [August, 1940.]

✉

[P.S.] MY DARLING, DEAR, BELOVED LITTLE ONES,

I know how you are — you are in the water a lot and you are well and you enjoy the healthful out-of-doors. Be very good and help your mother because you are already big girls. If only I could be with you and hug you until you scream so I'd let go. And then I'd squeeze you again. And don't forget the Czech language because if with God's help we can be together, we will understand each other. Now you'll start school again, and I wish you lots and lots of luck. Start out on the right foot. Now my darling Rayushka is starting first grade, and my darling Helgichka will go to third grade and before long Tomichek will follow you because he'll soon be two and I hope he'll be very healthy and will grow up to be a pleasure to his parents. And you, my darling girls, you will also be good and healthy and celebrate your mother's birthday, I will write again before the birthday because there is time. Oh, if only we could come soon.

✉

Jewish children were barred from public schools in the Protectorate. [August, 1940.]

✉

Letter 45   Nurembergstrasse 32
From Paula   Prague
                                                August 7, 1940

MY DEAR DARLING GOLDEN CHILDREN,

We received your third letter, of July 5, and we were happy with it. Now it's more than a year since we've seen you – who could have imagined it would be this long? And how much longer still it will be, only God knows. Mrs Wolff was here and said she would write you – did she? She thinks she'll be with you soon. I envy her, but I'm happy for her. I don't get out much because I don't have a maid, but maybe it's good and I'm glad God gives me the strength to do my work. It surprised me that my darling girls' tonsils were operated on – thank God it went well. They are so golden and dear to me. I understand that everyone likes them – it couldn't be any different. If only I could do something nice for them – and for my big kids too. On Sunday I was in Radovice – I wanted to know what Edith wrote. She writes that you have a nice apartment, that the kids already speak good English, that Tomichek is darling – and that Moshko wants a job in a hotel!? Shishinko doesn't tell me whether she has any help, so I worry about that. What can we do from far away? If only we could be together!

What we are doing, you can probably imagine. I have lots to do in the house, and Erwin has to fill his time too. That cannot really be described. We talk a lot about you and I see you in my dreams. I dreamed of you exactly the day before your letter came, and I thought I was already in the USA. In the dream I went home with you to your apartment,

Shishinko, and then we said goodbye and I went home again and I cried. I woke up thinking it meant something good — and then the letter came! And yesterday again we were all together — I love to see you in my dreams. I can't wait until it really happens. Moshko's mother is here with us often. She looks very well. Today she was here again, and sends kisses and greetings to all of you, but she doesn't feel like writing. As I have written you already, she's afraid you wouldn't be able to read it because she cannot write in Hebrew.

August 11, 1940
So, I left this letter lying here and today came your dear letter of July 29 — so now the mail goes fast. I'm so happy to hear from you. My thoughts are with you — God should make everything good for you. I pray for my children as soon as I wake up, before I even half open my eyes, I hope God hears me. I'm happy for you and happy you're there even while I miss you so. Did you receive two letters before this one? Today's letter was the fourth from you.

✉

Paula went to Radovice to visit her sister
Rosa Vogl.

Max, above all was flexible, and his
ability to improvise was tested at an early
age. His father, an itinerant cantor, fled
Russia to escape conscription in the

Russian army, in which Jews were forced to serve twenty-five year terms. Max's three brothers had already emigrated to Vienna, where they worked as opera singers. At the age of thirteen, Max undertook the trek to Prague with his mother and three sisters, acting as protector and breadwinner. They arrived in 1914. Max was instrumental in bringing the rest of his scattered family together, including his father, who had been caught by the Russians and sentenced to be executed but was subsequently ransomed by the Jewish Community.

Though he arrived as a penniless refugee, Max's resourcefulness continued to see him through. He had always had a flair for languages; ultimately, he became fluent in five and proficient in nine. He was befriended by a man who got him a tutoring job which, together with more menial work such as shining shoes, eventually enabled him to attend Charles University in Prague. There he earned a master's degree in economics, met Erwin and, consequently, Irma.

Max began work at Shell Oil through a

fluke: en route to an interview with another company, he accidentally got off on Shell's floor, talked his way into an interview, and got a job. He subsequently worked his way up through the company, eventually becoming General Manager. In America, when his life was turned upside down once again, Max took business courses at night at Northwestern University. He sold insurance and later went to work in the steel business. Eventually he started a steel brokerage firm, Atlas Metal Products, which did quite well. When his son Thomas decided against working at the firm, choosing instead to become a physician, Max dissolved his company and worked for other steel firms. He retired in 1983 at the age of eighty-one.

✉

To Prague

Letter 46   5335 Kimbark Avenue
From Max   Chicago, Illinois
To Paula and Erwin   September 1, 1940

MY DEARS,

We received your August 7 letter one day before we moved from St. Louis and we were very happy to have news from you again. As long as God grants good health, one must tolerate the hard times with patience and hope. In the meantime, we moved to Chicago. Last week I brought the family here. We have a very nice apartment that Irma found (Edith stayed for one day with the children so that Irma could come apartment-hunting in Chicago). Chicago is much nicer and more pleasant than St. Louis in every respect: the weather is better, the children have a beach, we don't live too far away – Irma has all available conveniences and the people are very nice, we already have some invitations, etc. Shell Oil closed its branch in St. Louis and I wanted to look for something else because hundreds of employees were let go. The president told me personally that he would like to keep me on, but if he did, the Americans who had worked for fifteen to twenty years in the same office would break his windows! In the end a deal was worked out with Shell in Chicago, although on a different level. Whether this will be better or worse, I don't know – only time will tell. The main thing is that, thank God we'll have enough to live on. But I think that in the long run it will turn out for the better – just as everything I was forced to do so far has turned out, "*toi toi toi.*" [Yiddish expression for "knock on wood."]

Anyway, Irma thinks so — and she should know. She is satisfied and will write you herself in more detail. Your decision to give up two rooms is a very good one, I think. Just as it is for Erwin to use his free time to learn other languages. I think Spanish is the best bet. As soon as possible, I will get in touch with the contacts here. A special thank you for the news that my people are well. I would like so much to get a direct sign of life from them. Couldn't they just write a few words in Czech? I enclose a letter. I would write her [Mother Czerner] directly but so far I have not gotten an answer to any of the direct letters — and second, where do they live now? Are they still in Bulharska [Street]? And, speaking of mothers, send regards to Frau Fleischmann. (I think at Pujckovny.) Her son Franta wrote me a letter, together with Armin and Regi (from London). They are all well, and so are Ella and Evichka.

✉

The "deal" with Shell "on a different level" meant that instead of the executive position he had held in St Louis, Max was now operating a gas station in a rough neighborhood on Chicago's South Side — pumping gas and changing spark plugs.

✉

Letter 47
From Max

5335 Kimbark Avenue
Chicago, Illinois
September 1, 1940

MY DEAREST MOTHER AND LOTTE AND ETTEL,

Why don't you write me a line? I wrote you so often and sent you pictures. Did you get all that? Thank God Mother Froehlich wrote me that you are well. That calms me down a bit, but write me at least a few lines, my dear Mama, it doesn't matter in which language. I want to see your handwriting and God willing, we will soon see each other again. And you, dear Lotte, write me a word. Write me — you, Mother and Lotte, how the matter of your immigration stands. The USA wrote me that the boat-tickets that I sent arrived but were never picked up and are no longer valid. Write me whether I should send more. Maybe send me a telegram and I will do anything. Please write me also whether you have enough to live on and where you now live.

Also: 1) Regarding the immigration, whether Lotte registered at the consulate and what kind of ticket I should send because the first ones expired and can no longer be used. And 2) Do you have enough to live on? Karl wrote me something about the Jewish Community. Do they pay you a pension, or should I do something and if so, what? 3) Where do you live? How is Lotte's foot? Don't think a day passes without my thinking of you. I think of you constantly, dearest Mother, how you sacrificed your whole life for us, how you traveled through all countries to get our documents and how we all left the nest and left you alone and in need. If I had known it would turn out this way I would rather have stayed with you; but after all, I could not work any more and I had to look after the children. And you yourself urged me to "go, already." And I've done everything to bring you here – if you had wanted you could already be here but unfortunately, dear Lotte could not get the visa that fast. We continue trying everything we can – and you try there. After all, Lotte is your child just as we are and I understand that you don't want to leave her alone and that creates all the problems. But I hope God gives us the strength to survive these hard times and that we'll see each other soon in peace, Amen.

Stay well, write me, even if only a few words. We are all, thank God, well. I am now in Chicago – not any more as well off as previously, but we're making it. Also, Janko, Elisha and Karl write that they are very happy. Karl will come here to Chicago soon, perhaps; I hope to get him a good job here. Just today he wrote a very nice letter. And if I can do anything: *Write me!*

Kisses and greetings for everybody: the Picks, the Poppers, Dolfens, etc. Frau Apteka wrote me recently.

✉

Max's comment on his mother's travel-ing through "all countries" to get docu-ments is a reference to her courageous, and perhaps clairvoyant, return to her native village in the early 1920s to secure birth-certificates for her whole family. Because of this, they could prove their Russian birth, and could enter the

USA under the Russian quota, which —
unlike the Czech quota — was wide
open.

The *Picks* were Hella's parents, Elisha's
in-laws; the *Poppers* were, as previously
mentioned, non-Jewish in-laws of Karl
Czerner's; *Frau Apteka* was Karl
Schnurmacher's mother-in-law, and
the *Dolfens* were Czech friends.

✉

Letter 48   Nurembergstrasse 32
From Paula   Prague
                                September 10, 1940

MY DEAR, PRECIOUS CHILDREN:

I think you are finished with your move, all of you are together in your new home, and I wish you all the best. Like a mother hen with her chickens, as you wrote, dear Shishinko, I want only the best for all of you. If only God, who is all powerful, fulfills all of my prayers — everything will turn out well for all of us. We are, thank God, well, and our thoughts fly to you. How are you, how do you feel? We also feel your thoughts winging toward us. Did you receive our last letter, in which we said it was our last letter to St. Louis? Now it is very close to Tommy's birthday! Please accept my warmest congratulations, Tommy and you too, Shisho — it would only be better if my eyes could see you and my hands touch you. Be well and happy and may God watch over you — if I could only tell you this in person and hand you a little present! But God has given you a greater gift than I could. And happy New Year — I wish you all the best — and you, dear Moshko, everything you want. Write us soon, everything about you. We cannot write much about ourselves, except how much we would love to be living with you. So — happy birthday for Tommy, and happy holidays. Be very happy, and feel very much loved by us. Erwinchek is very well and sends you all his love. Let's hope God lets everything work out well. I only want us all to be very happy. I love you very much.

                                          MAMA

My dear, sweet little girls:

So you are now going to a new school! Do you like your new classmates and teachers? And new friends? Who are your favorites? How much we think of you, and how nice it was to have you here with us! We must hope that God will make it be once more. Now I think of you as big girls. We smile to remember how your uncle kicked the ball to you. Maybe it will be once more. How nice it would be if we could all hug one another. I love you and kiss you.

Your Grandma

✉

Jews were banned from all but two Prague hotels. Jews were prohibited also from entering Prague's public wooded areas. [September, 1940.]

✉

Letter 49   Nurembergstrasse 32
From Erwin   Prague
                                                        September 1940

DEAR IRMA & MOSHKO,

I promised you a real long letter, and only today, after receiving your first letter from Chicago have I been able to get around to it. Most of all I wish you good luck in the new apartment and in the new big city. Also, best wishes for the holidays and for your birthday, dear Irma. Now I can tell you: Mother just had an operation done by Docent Klein in Sanatorium Borufka because of a uterine prolapse which has given her trouble for many years and had become much worse lately. She very bravely made the decision, so that she can be well and stay with us in good health for another hundred years. I highly recommended the surgery and she came through it very well, and now that it is over I can tell you and you need not worry. The last work she did before she went to the hospital was to write to you, and her last walk was to the post office to mail that letter; right after that, I accompanied her to the sanatorium. She was operated on the next day and had to stay for two weeks. Thank God she had no fever nor the usual urinary nor bowel problems. Now Mother is home again and must stay at bed-rest for another week on doctor's orders. She looks very well and some good people take care of her. A neighbor cooks and brings her the midday meal and a cleaning woman comes in the morning. Every day, she improves. Today Mrs Fleischmann visited and she was very happy with your letter. Mrs Wolff visited her in the hospital.

Today I met Mr Gross and he also sends his regards. When mother is fully recovered, in approximately two weeks, a couple with a seven-year-old boy will move in with us. We rented two rooms to this couple because, as you know, I no longer need a whole four-room apartment and we will manage with two. It will also decrease the work of maintenance. You don't need to worry, dear Moshko, about your mother. Even if she doesn't write you, she repeatedly asks me for your address. She is just as healthy as she has always been and she has enough to live on. She visits us more often, and she still lives in Bulharska, Vrsovice district. About me, nothing new or interesting to tell you.

Dr Sperling wrote yesterday, announcing the opening of his practice.

LOVE AND KISSES,
ERWIN

DEAR HELGICHKO AND RAYUSHKO,

You will be readers like your uncle — you will be very smart girls, because every year you move to another street and another city and another school: in Prague, in St. Louis and now in Chicago. You will like it there very much, and you will definitely become doctors for your dolls. Grandma would like to give you a kiss again — and Uncle also. Love to Tommy. Who tells you stories?

A MILLION KISSES,
YOUR UNCLE

Letter 50
From Paula

Nurembergstrasse 32
Prague
September 1940

MY DEAR, SWEET, ROUND LITTLE CHILDREN:

Maybe you can't even read this any more — have you forgotten Czech or not? No, don't! What would I do, you couldn't even talk to me? What's happening with the piano? Can you play well enough now so I can dance to your music? And Tomichek would be my partner. You know, little ones, when I miss you the most I take out your pictures and look at you — but I know you look different now, and that's why I would like more pictures. And what are you doing, my darling Helgichka? Do you help your mother? You must be a big girl already. And you, my darling Rayushka, do you remember us? I see you children before me all the time. You put on plays — and I have put up your drawings and I enjoy looking at them. And you, my little golden Tomichek, you made big eyes at me but you didn't understand me. Be well, my darlings. Kisses!

YOUR BABICHKA

Letter 51   Nurembergstrasse 32
From Paula   Prague
                                                        October 7, 1940

MY DEAR PRECIOUS CHILDREN:

Just today on your birthday, we received your letter which
was written September 19th. You are right, dear Moshko, that
I can't read it without tears but in front of Erwin I have to
suppress them because he doesn't like to see me cry. But these
are tears of joy, because I have heard from you again. As long
as I know you are in good health; if only I could help a little with
all the work, especially Shishinko's. I would like to help Moshko
too, but I don't know how to do his work. What can we do?
We have to hope that with God's help things will change and
we'll all meet in happiness. Very often I recall how a lady said,
in front of Raya, "We must have hope." And then my darling
Rayushka said, "First hope — then despair." [In Czech, this
rhymes.] So I keep remembering different things that my dear
little girls used to say. It was so nice when I could hug and kiss
them. But I hold on to the conviction that all will end well.
Don't worry, I am healthy and in good spirits. I often chat
with you in my imagination, but I have to watch myself so that
I don't get carried away; also I see you before me always, and
dream of you often. How did you celebrate your [Irma's]
birthday? Did you get our birthday greetings? When I was in
the hospital, I imagined my dear little girls dancing around my
bed, and it was so lively! Did you find some household help
yet? Especially, Shishinko, help with heavy work? I'm glad that
you have a nice apartment and that you like it there better than
in St. Louis and that the darling girls have a shorter walk to

school, but I don't like to hear that Rayushka eats poorly! Maybe a doctor could give her something to improve her appetite. Here, also, her poor appetite troubled me and I tried very hard with her. My dear Helgichka ate better and was more cheerful. Just ask her how I felt younger when both of them were in good moods.

But now they are both content. Edith wrote about them, how darling they are, especially Tomichek. But the worst part for her was the physical work. Wouldn't it be possible to find someone to work for room and board only? Maybe an immigrant? Here, one can often find someone to do housework in exchange for bed and breakfast. I would do it here if I had available space. I have to clean up my things because I have to cram them all into two rooms. I would like to have it all in order already. And since the surgery I have to go slowly but thank God it's behind me. I had all that bladder trouble, and with winter coming it would have gotten worse. Mrs Wolff visited me often in the hospital. I sent a note to Mrs Fleischmann and she also came right away and still does, she is very nice. If only Franta would write her a line or two! Moshko, can't you get him to write? Does Regi write you often? How are they? Did you receive the letter to which I added a note from your mother? I admire the American schools, how the children learn everything, even music and singing. I would so like to sit on the bench with Tomichek in the pram next to me, but all I can do is imagine it from what dear Moshko writes. Because I no longer spend time on my grooming I look so terrible that people would laugh if they saw me but that wouldn't matter if we could only be together. I'm jumping around in this letter, again! Give the children little open-faced sandwiches [a Czech treat] and things from the bakery, especially Raya, because these are what she used to like to eat. They had their favorites here. Also give them butter, it's probably healthy. They like butter and honey very much. [Last few lines are torn and illegible.]

[Note in margin] There should be many girls who would be happy to live with a family rent-free and do some work in the house. So, I kiss you and greet you.

YOUR LOVING MOTHER

Letter 52
From Erwin

Nurembergstrasse 32
Prague
October 8, 1940

DEAR IRMA AND MOSHKO,

As you can see from Mother's letter, she is perfectly okay. I hope you received our letter of October 1. After much effort, I was able to get an unpaid position as a "psychological technician," so now I am occupied. It is a very nice field. I do the Rorschach and other tests. It is in the building where we live and under the direction of Mr Schonfeld, so it's convenient. It's possible that later on I'll get paid. In addition, I'm taking a course in psychology. Many doctors are in that course. Because I'm busy all day, I can only progress in my language studies on my own: English, Spanish and Russian. That has to suffice!

Stay well and be happy.

CORDIALLY,
YOUR ERWIN

DEAREST KIDS —

You will have to wait a little longer for the promised stories!

KISSES,
YOUR UNCLE

Letter 53   Nurembergstrasse 32
From Paula   Prague
November 8, 1940

MY DEAR, DARLING, GOLDEN PRECIOUS CHILDREN:

It seems forever since you wrote. The last letter from you came just on your birthday, my dear Shishinko, and we answered immediately. Now we wait for the mailman to bring us another letter but so far nothing. I called your mother, Moshko, and she had no letter either. We always call each other when we get a letter. Your mother tells me that Elisha wrote lately that you, dear Moshko, have established yourself independently and this surprised me very much because I thought you had stayed with the firm. I hope it goes well. God should grant you health and happiness. Good luck in all of your undertakings: I would like to hear from you — that, for me, would be the best thing. That, and that we should be well and together. The whole truth, Shishinko darling, is that I wish I could have gone with you only I didn't want to hold you up — but I am glad for you, and Erwin is too. Now we look forward to letters. If only dear God would bring peace so we could be together again. If only times were better. We have had to take people in again. We gave up two rooms for four people, but there were only three people so they had to take someone in. I have a tiny little kitchen and both families cook there, and the pots and pans are being stolen. But we have to cook, so we go marketing at eleven in the morning to get the meal ready. But we get along very well and do the dishes together — one washes and the other dries. And so it goes.

MAMA

In November 1940, Jews were not allowed to leave their city of residence without special permission from the Zentralstelle.

Letter 54   Nurembergstrasse 32
From Erwin   Prague
                                              December 2, 1940

DEAR IRMA & MOSHKO,

We were very happy with your last letter and the
packet shipped via Bremen — you have already been
informed it arrived and have our thanks for it. We are well
— no change. Mother is recovering nicely from her surgery,
no complications, only she cannot go for walks and fresh air
because she is too busy, cooking in the same kitchen as her
"boarders," which is not very pleasant. We now have four
"boarders," and we hope that we don't get any more
"growth" because we are already cramped enough. What I
am doing, I already wrote you — in contrast to you, Moshko,
who don't tell me about yourself! I hope you found a good
job in Chicago. You, dear Irma, needn't be overly im-
pressed with my great knowledge of psychotherapeutic
technique — the only use for it is in my work as an
employment counselor, for which I am not paid; at least I
have something to do, and see people. But there is not the
slightest chance that I will get paid for it — not even a little
pocket money — but I hope that this is not all wasted time,
since every now and then I do study gastroenterology if only
the theoretical aspects. There is so much to be learned; but
I often lack enthusiasm because I don't even know what I
should study, or even in what language. In my profession
especially, the opportunities are the worst. I had your
mother, Moshko, test me in Russian; I read to her and there

was only an occasional word that she had to translate for me. Now she looks better than ever. Recently we had a visit from Mr Wolff — he says he wrote you too. He was surprised at how grey I am getting.

BEST REGARDS, LOVE AND KISSES,
ERWIN

It is likely that Erwin's work as an "employment counselor" consisted of classifying people for work at the Jewish Community, by order of the Germans.

Letter 55   5335 Kimbark Avenue
From Irma   Chicago, Illinois
To an ex–neighbor in St. Louis   [Date unknown]

DEAR MR AND MRS BERGER,

We hope very much that you and your lovely children are all right. Although there is not much time for us left for writing we still think and speak of you very often and regret that we could not continue to be your neighbors.

This time I have a very special and for myself most important reason for writing you. There is some possibility now for my mother and brother to get here if they have an affidavit. We are of course sending them ours but in addition to that we need one from American friends. We also had found somebody who was willing to take care of that but unfortunately he got ill and is not able to do it now. As time is a very important factor in this matter we are afraid to wait any longer and so I ask you – knowing your outstanding kindness – would you do me this very very great favor to sign an affidavit for them? I hope you know us well enough to be assured that it would be a mere formality and that we are able and more than willing to support them.

Maybe if you try to place yourself in a similar position you would feel how greatly I would appreciate a positive reaction to my demand and how very grateful I would be.

And would it please be possible for you to let me have your answer without delay, excuse me if it sounds unmodest but time has become so precious that I would even ask you to send a cable on our expense, hoping that you will understand and excuse my impolite hurry. (affidavit enclosed)

The dates are:

Paula Froehlich born October 4, 1876 in Rokicany, Bohemia.

Erwin Froehlich, M.D. born March 18, 1903 in Prague, Bohemia.

Their address now is:

Prague V, Nurembergstrasse 32.

We are looking forward to your answer and send the very sincerest regards to both of you and to Gloria and Nancy, also from Helga and Raya and Tommy (he is a little man already).

YOURS,
IRMA CZERNER

Affidavits, at this point, could evidently be supplied by American citizens who were *not* relatives.

To Prague

Letter 56
From Irma

5335 Kimbark Avenue
Chicago
January 2, 1941

MY DEAR MOTHER AND ERWIN,

Again I waited so long for your letter, and I feel like a new person since I got it! It caresses me, and I breathe a sigh of relief. I am thankful that at least we can correspond. If only God grants that you stay well, and that we can be reunited in joy.

Your letter came just on New Year's Eve, so it must be a good omen for the New Year; so my appetite is restored as the year begins well. At the same time we got a letter from the Wolffs. They also write about you: that they visited with you and that you, dear mother, are still a sharp and elegant lady! I'm picturing it! I'm going to read that part over again! Only, dear mother, don't be a fuss-budget — the world will go on even if you miss dusting one day! And instead, lie down and rest a bit— or read something. (Kathe will be glad to lend you some books — she has a lot.) And if your "boarders" are otherwise pleasant, overlook their faults, and talk to them. Do you take turns cleaning up the kitchen? We are very happy that you received the package in good condition. We know how it is there, so Max chose those things for you and for his mother. We thought that she wouldn't eat sausages and similar things. How is Lotte? Ettel? I always wanted to ask you, do you have a phone? What is the number? Ours is Midway 5840.

I meant to write you back right away on New Year's Eve, but I didn't because Moshko got me a small portable radio just when your letter came, and I took it into the kitchen with me and it gave me such a lift I really felt like working. Midnight — the New Year — arrived, and then I was too tired.

For New Year's we were invited, with the children, to some friends. (They were at our house a week ago and brought us a pretty little potty-chair for Tomichek.) They live at the other end of Chicago, and it is an hour by train. They brought us back by car, and it also took more than an hour. Tomichek liked that very much. Tomichek said "bye bye" when he saw the train! On the way home he slept. It's really cute the way he talks. He mixes it up: Czech with us, and English with the kids. The *zaby* [frogs— a playful reference to the girls] are forgetting Czech, but I teach them. At home I make them speak Czech because at school they have enough English. They both, thank God, look well and the main thing is that they are healthy and lively.

No, dear mother, I am not moving to New York. Elisha put a bug in your ear! Moshko will write you. At least, dear mother, you'll be happy again knowing that we are staying here in Chicago. You are right that it is better here than in New York, and thank God, we make a living, and we enjoy the lake and the beach. Oh mother, I look at it always through your eyes — you would like it too. Moshko and I go downtown and there we really feel we are in America and look at everything wide-eyed.

Now we have "the little devils" at home because they have a two-week Christmas vacation from school, so they enjoy Tomichek and are wild with him. You can't imagine the noise but, thank God, most of the time I can tolerate it and in general they are very good. They play all the time with "their" (my) gramophone. I bought them the records from *Snow White* and they play them from morning to night. And Tommy always runs in and asks me, "Do you hear 'heigh-ho, heigh-ho'?" Or

"Do you hear 'I'm vishin' ['I'm wishing']!" and he sings it to the girls. Now we are lying on our bellies on the sofa, and Tommy is drawing and rolling his eyes. And, oh, Maminko — I see you with us and I hear you calling me "ah, Shishinko," in my heart.

Tommy got a train for Channukah — but the children wrote you about that already. The girls got long robes. Here, one wears long housecoats at home. They are cheap, but they're nothing, I don't care to wear them for housework. They look like curtains — they have flowers and pleats. At least, though, the girls change into them when they come home from school to play with Tomichek, so they don't bring germs home from school and their school clothes don't get so dirty. In winter they wear what they call snowsuits here. They're very practical, and the children don't have to toughen up with bare knees in the cold weather.

The children were so happy that you wrote. And Helgichka said, "If only my arms were long enough to put around her and pull her to me." Helga talked about how it looked in Zbraslav, and Raya remembered how Erwin didn't want to change into his bathing suit and then a boat came by and splashed him and he got wet.

This month was Papa's *yahrzeit*. We lit the *yahrzeit* candle and then the children told his picture everything that they remembered about their grandpa.

A *yahrzeit* candle is burned for 24 hours to commemorate the anniversary of a family member's death. This is a universal Jewish custom, although it is not universally customary to burn the candle in front of a picture of the deceased, as was done here.

Letter 57   Nurembergstrasse 32
From Paula   Prague
                                   February 16, 1941

MY DEAR SWEET CHILDREN,

We have just received your dear letter of 3 December. We were wondering why you were not writing us, but nobody had any mail from America — I think it was the fault of the mail service. I am most, most happy and thankful to God that you are all healthy — as are we. I hope you got our letter thanking you for the package. I thank you in every letter, because if one letter got lost you wouldn't know the package arrived. From Edith and Arnold you know that Aunt Rosa and Erna may be going soon to join them — I think maybe in April. I envy them, but am also happy for them. And I think . . . well, you know.

I hear that you are totally Americanized. Just now under our window (I'm writing at the window) I saw two little girls with their mother about like Helgichka and Rayushko — but now they would be bigger. So I had to stop writing and look at them. It hurts so much. One family that lives with us has boys. One is eight years old. He sometimes calls me Babushinko, as my dear little girls did, and he says, "Do you think it's your Helgichka and Rayushka?" I am always talking to everyone about you. He says, "I am also your grandson," and kisses me, and would like to be around me all the time — but he cannot compensate. His mother says I'm like her mother and she is like my daughter — but nobody can take the place of my Shishinko. When I think of my little girls I cry. If only I knew where and when I will see them. I never thought it would be this long, when you said we would be together soon. My dear Tomichek must be a fine chap — how could it be otherwise? His Mommy and Daddy are so wonderful! How happy I am that the children sing songs, and how I love to hear stories about them. I read the letters so often, but then I cry. I wish I wouldn't cry, but that's me! Did you, dear Moshko, get our congratulations for your birthday? Happy birthday. God willing, we will tell it to you in person. Your dear Mother is well, and we now have good relations with Lotte — and with E. [Ettel?] also, so everything is okay. Did you get the letter that Lotte wrote to all of you? Do you have anyone to help you (at home) yet? Are you going to move?

Now two families live with us, but I have no trouble from them. We live in one room so at least I have little work to do — but there's always something that needs doing. At least we are well, and you are too. I hear that now brothers and sisters can vouch for each other, so maybe Erwin can also get an affidavit from you? Now I want to write to my darling children, so I will close. Rabl always asks about you. He now runs around a lot. Faninka has a lot of trouble with him. We sometimes go and see Uncle Rudy and Aunt Elsa. Aunt Clara, as I wrote you, is now alone — Uncle Louis died. She would like to come here. So, much love to all of you — be well and happy.

MANY KISSES, YOUR MAMINKA.

Did my darling little girls have their tonsils out?

Rules for affidavits kept changing. Paula's

comment that brothers and sisters can now "vouch for each other" — meaning supply affidavits — may reflect some confusion on her part, as well as the lack of current information in Prague at this time on U.S. immigration policy.

Letter 58   Nurembergstrasse 32
From Erwin   Prague
                                        February 17, 1941

[DEAR MAX AND IRMA,]

    I thank you for your letter. You make too much of my attentiveness to dear Mama after her operation. The most important thing is that she made her mind up so quickly and decisively to allow the operation. She feels quite well and would have suffered more without the operation. Now we have only one room; there is Mama with me, and naturally the furniture is quite disorganized. Nevertheless, the room looks quite nice. I continue to work in the Psychotechnical Clinic, and participate in a course on employment counseling. I don't study much anymore, including language, because there is always somebody coming in who takes up my time.

ERWIN

DEAR CHILDREN,

I send many greetings and kisses and bedtime stories. I have not forgotten the bedtime stories — and when I have a chance I surely will write. Stay well, all of you. We are so glad to get letters from you.

HEARTFELT LOVE,
ERWIN

✉

*Jews were required to turn in driving
licenses and forbidden to take driving
lessons. [January, 1941.]*

✉

Letter 59   Nurembergstrasse 32
From Paula   Prague
                                February 28, 1941

MY DEAREST, DARLING CHILDREN,

I hope you have received mail from us recently, because in one letter was a note from Lotte, asking for boat tickets; did you get it? I also wrote you in my last letter for an affidavit for Erwin because it is rumored that children, parents and also sisters and brothers can request them. Today I ask you to do for us as much as you can so that we can come to you and so that our long-hoped-for reunion might be possible. It is said that boat tickets can be sent by wire, and that we would be notified by the consulate in Vienna. We would be so grateful and would repay you a thousandfold if you could do that. Erna says that Edith has helped her accomplish everything so far, and that the help has to come from over there, so therefore I beg you urgently to do your utmost. Erwin has written to Vienna, and your letter from January 2 we just got yesterday. Your dear mother, Moshko, I notified immediately and she came over. I urged her with all my heart that she should try to join you — she would like for us to go together. She claims that Lotte is very good and that Ettel now lives in a home so it is very quiet in her house. So your mother doesn't have to get so angry now.

Many thanks for the snapshots, we are very happy to get them, but why not two copies of each? I would have loved to keep the one with Moshko and Tomichek but couldn't pull it off. After all, I can't be so greedy. I pressed the pictures to my lips and to my heart. Tomichek is very big and beautiful, and he looks strong. Rayushka seems to have grown a lot but she has skinny legs and she looks very thin. And on the pictures she looks angry — was she mad about something? And my Helgichka is very big, and soon both of them will be as tall as you. The phone we will have, perhaps for a few days or maybe till the end of March. One needs it very, very rarely. The number is 64467. Tante Steffi is now very nasty but we try to get by. Therefore, once more, I urgently ask you to do everything and write by return mail. Yesterday I wrote you, and Lotte and your mother said they wrote you. I always tell them to write you and they always promise me.

BEST WISHES AND MANY KISSES,

MAMA

✉

The reference to Ettel being "in a home" may mean that she was in some kind of mental institution. She was extremely unstable and she and Mother Czerner had difficulty living together.

Residential telephones were disconnected except for those of lawyers, doctors and midwives. [January, 1941.]

A year later, Jews were forbidden to use public telephones of any kind. Phones of non-Jews sharing a house with Jews were disconnected.

✉

[P.S. MY DEAR LITTLE ONES,]

We were so happy with your sweet letter and your pictures; at least it's possible to kiss you if only on the picture. But I think you, my Rayushinko, eat poorly — you have such skinny little legs — Helgulatko I do not see, she is standing behind her Mommy, so I can't tell. So — Tommy shouldn't be ashamed of you. If only your arms were long enough, dear Helgichka, if they were long enough to bring us to you, that's what we wish. Pray that God will bring it about soon. That would be so wonderful. Shishinko, don't work so hard, look around for someone to help you.

BABICHKA

Letter 60
From Paula

Nurembergstrasse 32
Prague
March 4, 1941

DEAREST CHILDREN,

Every day I wait for a letter from you and I go crazy waiting for the mailman. I jump so that I'm right at the door when he rings. I hope you are all well. You have had many letters from us, hope you received them all. Mother is often here and sends her regards. I must write her and tell her you are all well. She would write, but she says she can't write — I want only her signature. Two weeks ago I wrote. She was glad to get the package — so were we. Every night we think of you — we eat a little from the package at every dinner — you are always with us in spirit when we eat. If only it were real! Aunt Rosa and Erna are in Vienna. Aunt Rosa already has a visa but they do not want to allow Erna to leave. (Something about Yugoslavia and some visa complication.) Can you send us new affidavits? Erwin wrote to Vienna but got no answer, but the affidavit must be no older than one year. You never wrote if you have help in the house. Thank God Moshko has a good job. You have no worries. I hope God will see to it that we are all together soon. In our neighborhood everything is okay. They like us — they are content — we feel at home — sometimes, they are helpful. Yesterday there was a lot of snow. This winter is very long, today it's sunny, but we don't have time for a walk to the river, where I would walk if I had time. Here, the dear children could not walk and pick flowers as they can there.

Please begin obtaining affidavits.

(Four days later) It rained all day and all night. Erna has

has her visa, so they both can go. Mrs Wolff called and he [Rolf] is no longer there. I'm sure she wrote you. Mrs Wolff is here in Prague now. I will go and see them.

So — good-bye and be well.

MAMA

✉

"He is no longer there": probably Rolf Wolff had been deported. "I will go and see them" – i.e. Kathe and Marion.

The comments about not having time for a walk to the river and the children not being able to walk and pick flowers probably refer to anti-Jewish restrictions then in effect.

Jews were not allowed on the banks of the River Moldau or in the vicinity of Hradcany Palace. They were specifically banned from public thoroughfares running through small parks in the center of the city. [Edicts issued in July, October, 1941 and January 1942.] There already was a law banning Jews from public parks and gardens in Prague.(See Letter 44n)

Certain main thoroughfares were declared off-limits to Jews from three p.m. Saturdays until eight a.m. on Mondays. [June, 1942.]

Paula's comment that she "must write Mother Czerner" must indicate that either one or both of these women no longer had a phone. In the past, Paula had telephoned Mother Czerner whenever she received a letter from the States.

Letter 61 Nurembergstrasse 32
From Paula Prague
My dear darling children, March 5, 1941

I hope you have recently received mail from us, because we have written you often lately. Also we have answered your last letter written January 2. Thank goodness you are in good health and we are too. If only God would grant that everything should be all right. If only we were as near to you as Erna and Tante Rosa! As Erna told us, they have Edith and Arnold to thank for doing everything for them over there. Erwin wanted to wire you about a ticket, but I didn't think that was necessary. Did you send the tickets? I only beg you, dear children, please do something for us — so that we have some hope of getting there. You cannot imagine how we long for you. Erwin is now very sad. I don't know how to write you about the situation. Please, please rescue us and send us the affidavits. Erwin also wrote to the consulate in Vienna.

You asked me, Shishinko, how it is with the lodgers: we cook together in a small kitchen and with few dishes — but we get along together. We wash the dishes and clean up together — eight people. The maid comes tomorrow — she helps clean up and then goes home. As for food, there is enough but it is very expensive. We pay her 330 Kr. for half a day and with health insurance that comes to 370 Kr. Laundry she does in her home. When it gets warmer and we don't have to pay for heat, it will be better. We're waiting for a speedy answer.

My dearest children, I am with you in spirit — be healthy and happy. Helgichka, the little stone I carry always in my wallet. Do you remember what you gave me? A little heart. I wouldn't give it away for anything. Send me some more pictures, we love them. When we get there, maybe Rayushka will already know how to play the piano and you too, Helgulatko. And dear Tomichek, when we come you will meet us at the train. So — many, many kisses to all of you — Your loving mother and grandmother. Also from Erwin, many kisses. He is not home and I want to mail this because I'm going shopping and I can mail this so that it goes — flies!

MAMA

✉

No female citizen under the age of 45 could accept employment in a household which included a Jewish adult; one already employed could remain if she was 35 years old by July 1, 1942. [March, 1942.]

Helga had given Paula a little pebble she found. It was shaped like a heart.

✉

Letter 62
From Paula

Nurembergstrasse 32
Prague
March 18, 1941

[MY DEAR CHILDREN,]

I'm writing you for the third time. It's impossible for me to finish a letter, I'm always interrupted and the paper gets torn up so you wouldn't be able to read it. So I'm writing again — thank you so very much for the package. I must tell you, we were expecting it because you said one was coming. It is so uplifting for us to feel your presence from so far — it is so hard for us here, we think that when we taste the good taste of what you send, we see you in spirit among us — but don't be angry if I tell you not to spend so much money on us, you need it there. The yellow I cooked right away, to preserve it, and the white also so as not to lose any. I still have one can of ham from you stashed away in my cupboard, and now I'm going to save the salami. Your mother, Moshko, also tasted it and said, "This is ham, this is not kosher," but she says it will give her strength and she also thanks you. So you can see that your mother eats everything. We've had several debates about this but now she listens to me. She looks very well. She would like to leave fast to be with you but Lotte weighs heavy on her heart. She does not want to leave her, so she is staying here. She won't budge on this, but she is hoping that Lotte can leave too.

If only God would grant all our wishes. It seems not two years, but a lifetime since we saw each other. I never thought that we would be apart for such a long time. When you left I thought, "There go my children, but within the year we'll be together again." After the girls left, it was such a long time and we are still here — but now we want to just fly to you and we long for you so — if the children were ill, Shishinko, I could help you, it must be so hard for you. If only I could help you, and if Erwin could help too and we could all be together. We could manage without any trouble and at night we would run to the children's rooms. Rosa and Erna already have their visas, God help them. We are in good health and I am glad that after my operation I am in good health and can walk very fast.

M<small>AMA</small>

✉

Nobody has any idea what food "the yellow" and "the white" could have been.

✉

To Prague

Letter 63
From Irma

5335 Kimbark Avenue
Chicago
[March 26], 1941

DEAR MAMA AND ERWINCHKO:

Your ears must always be ringing because I am always thinking of you, and I'm always wondering, will there be a letter from you today? It's so long since we heard from you. If only you are well! I have a picture here of the *Stare Mesta*, and oh, how I would love to jump into it and turn the corner and run to see you! That would be something! How we would grab each other around the neck and hug each other, no? And what gossip and stories we'd tell! If only God will make it happen soon! That's what we all hope over here. Just stay well and persevere.

So, my darlings, what are you doing? I can only hope that I will get news of you soon. Do you have our last letter with birthday wishes to you, dear Erwin? It will soon be spring — the sun is already warming up. (Yesterday, there was still snow.) I only hope the sun is shining on you and warming you too. If only we could all be together! Did you get the second package? I hope you already ate it in good health. I'm glad that your cold is better. I didn't write you how warm it is here — and so cold there. I only hope you're well. Here, there is nothing new. The little children are, thank God, well — and your "big children" are also well. We are very busy, and it does us good. Sometimes we go to a movie, when we have a woman to watch the children — but, you know, "social butterflies," as we were in Prague, we are no longer! And oh, how I'd love to show you Chicago. When I go downtown with Moshko, I make him pretend he's you — "Look, Mama," I say, " what do you think of that?" And he always has to say something that you would say. He says: "Now, *that* I never expected in America!" And he imitates Erwin too: "Ohh — nice!" And I want to tell you something else, Mama: now that I have to do all my own housework and cooking and take care of the children, I can't tell you how much I admire you for how well you did it, and how far I still am from your example. You know, the children are pretty good — but sometimes they get me mad. But "kids will be kids." Last week they brought home report cards from school — all top grades, and very good comments from the teachers.

Last week they had a Purim festival at Raya's Sunday School class (they go to Sunday School every Sunday; religion is not taught in regular school). I sewed her a costume and she was happy. The children have lots of friends, and after school they go to friends' homes or bring friends home. Right now they have some little girls here visiting. I gave them some ice cream and Tommy is with them, so I have a little peace to write. Oh — they just brought Tommy back because he wet his pants. It's hard to toilet-train boys — do you have any advice for me?

I hope Armin can come here soon, perhaps in two months — it would be good to live near each other. We must cross our fingers. From New York, we hear that Tante Steffi will not last long but she just seems to go along; Elisha is a cantor in Pittsburgh — we have already written you that. Janko moved to another neighborhood, so there is only Karl at the old address. Just yesterday we got the receipt for a package from Lotte — from you, not as yet. It went via Japan!

I would love to be able to tell you when we will see each other — but in the meantime, stay well.

MUCH, MUCH, LOVE.
YOUR SHISHA

Stare Mesta is the name of the oldest section of Prague, close to the Jewish cemetery, near Paula's pre-war apartment.

Purim was celebrated on March 18th in 1941. This was also Erwin's birthday.

In Prague, Irma had relied on servants to do the housework and cooking, and was free to concentrate on her artistic interests. Just before she left Prague she had been commissioned to illustrate a children's book. In addition, she had had the foresight to design several pieces of compact furniture for America, where she knew she would be living in smaller quarters. These pieces were produced and shipped, and are still being used by the family. In America, despite her increased family responsibilities, she still found time to be creative; she designed and made all her children's clothes, sold some of her decorative artwork to Marshall Field & Company and continued to paint all her life.

To Prague

Letter 64
From Irma

5335 Kimbark Avenue
Chicago
[March ?], 1941

MY DEAR MOTHER,

I am very happy with your letter, and glad to know that you received the package and that it tasted good and that you are in good health. You know, Maminko, that since I last wrote you, Moshko has another job. He just telephoned to surprise me, and we will have to move if it comes through, but I'm sorry to say that for the time being he doesn't earn much because, as I wrote you, he had to take a cut in salary. Right now they are not accepting applications so we have only enough money for necessities. Now you have received the affidavits. We are happy that, in any case, we now have some hope that we can bring you over. At least we can hope for it and work for it.

You know that Aunt Rosa is very opinionated — and she likes to brag about Edith and everything that she can accomplish. She never really told you how easy it was for them, compared with our situation. She never told you that an apartment is ready for them for sure, that Arnold was busy making plans for their arrival even before Moshko and I left, and that Edith has had a job since she and Arnold got here; and I learned from others that they have other connections too, and plenty of money. Edith wrote me that their boat tickets have been paid for since December. We couldn't do that. We are in a different situation. The quota was closed for at least the next four years.

Edith wrote too that she hopes they will get to the ship in time. She expects them to arrive at the boat the first of April. They should be on the train four weeks before the sailing date – that would be April 18, but Edith herself is having a very difficult time getting them out, so we hope God will help. I hope you too will get here as soon as possible.

And now I will tell you something that will interest you: we found our relatives and they are sending you affidavits! There were pages and pages with that name in the telephone book, but we still found them! They are youngsters – Fred is 35, Richard 27. So far we have only met Fred. They live with their mother about an hour and a half from us by train. Their mother is sick and housebound. So far we haven't gone out to see them, but we've talked to them on the phone. They invited us to come and see them after they move the first of May. They speak Czech and English – English a bit better. Both are working, and in the evening keep house and cook because their mother is sick. Fred is small, thin, and not very handsome, and smart though not very educated – and he is very nice to the children. The main thing is that we hope he will take care of the affidavits this week and that I will be able to send them to you with this letter.

✉

The "other connections" that Irma mentions probably refer to Edith's friendship with Eleanor Roosevelt. [See p. 204] She is apparently responding to Paula's desperate comments in *Letter 61* about Edith and Arnold working so hard to get Aunt Rosa and Erna to the U.S.

The relatives, Fred and Richard Froehlich, whose mother was Aunt Julia, were related to Irma's paternal great-uncle. As it developed, these people never provided affidavits. They seemed cold and indifferent to the plight of Czech Jews and to the gravity of the situation, which Irma undoubtedly conveyed to them.

✉

Letter 65
From Erwin

Nurembergstrasse 32
Prague
[April] 1941

DEAR IRMICKA AND MOSHKO,

We had been waiting a long time for a letter, and were very happy to get a long one. We thank you for trying so hard, and maybe your endeavors will result in a trip for us. From here we can do nothing. The consulate doesn't even give us an answer. In any case, it can only help if you send us an affidavit. Aunt Rosa and Erna are sitting and waiting to leave, even though everything is in order. We were very pleasantly surprised that you were able to find our aunt and cousins in Chicago. You are so clever! They were so nice to you! We send them greetings. Did I ever write to Fred and Richard? Here there are no changes. Dear mother has a lot of housework and must do everything herself except for a cleaning woman who comes three times a week. I spend my day in the Department of Psychiatry so that I have something to do. It's quite interesting — of course, I don't get paid for it at all. The working hours begin at seven a.m. We love working with the children; some of my colleagues would have loved to do prophylactic psychoanalysis with Helgichka and Rayushka. We will try to send you a picture. I hope that in your new apartment you won't have such a hot summer as last year. You could take the family on trips around Chicago. I'm sure you now have a large circle of friends and acquaintances. Do you go to the museum with the children?

I have to close now and miss you all.

ERWIN

It was believed in some circles that
"prophylactic," or early, psychoanalysis
of children would prevent the develop-
ment of adult neuroses, resulting from
childhood trauma.

Letter 66
From Paula

Nurembergstrasse 32
Prague
May 5, 1941

MY DEAR SWEET CHILDREN,

We got your letter of March 26, and then right away we got another saying you had been with Teta Froehlich, and we were very glad. I grabbed the letter from the mailman and hugged it and cried with pleasure. It had been so long since we heard anything from you. Thank God you are all well and happy. If only we could be together soon, but I don't really believe any more that it will happen. Rosa and Erna were to leave this Sunday, but their departure has been postponed for one week. We have had no answer from Vienna, and I hear that for every step we must have a new affidavit, so please write to the consul in Vienna quickly and tell him that new and current affidavits are ready for us. We must also have boat tickets ready but even with these we must wait till the end of the year to depart — and it is better if we have the possibility of getting the boat passage from the U.S.; to buy it here is very, very expensive. Here, every week the USA changes the immigration regulations. You have better access to new information about it than we. From the boat ticket, we would know which month we could leave, but new and current affidavits would be necessary. The Wolffs want to leave this week. It's hard for me to get out of the house. In the morning I have much to do, and in the afternoon by the time the kitchen is cleaned up [illegible]. I'm so glad I have the yellow from you. I warmed it to save it, but we ate the second batch right away. I wanted to save it, but I was afraid it would spoil. If we could be together we could go for a walk together, my dear Shishinko, as you wrote, to the center of town and be all together, how happy we would be. I'm so glad the dear little ones are studying and learning so well, but I pray they are also very good at home — but I can't even believe that they wouldn't be!

✉

Teta Froehlich is Aunt Julia, the mother of Fred and Richard, mentioned in *Letter 63*.

See *Letter 62* and *note* for earlier reference to "yellow".

✉

Letter 67
From Paula

Nurembergstrasse 32
Prague
May 1941

MY DEAREST CHILDREN,

You really make me smile, Shishinko: so Raya wheedled a Purim costume out of you! I would love to see a picture! Again I see from your letter that I've written you very often. And now, regarding Tomichek — all in all, there's nothing you can do about it — he'll learn. Maybe he can't hold it, and pants are very complicated! But now summer is coming so it won't be so bad. Most children wet themselves until age three. How I wish Erwin and I could be among you! Why was it decided that Armin will live with you in your apartment? Your mother, Moshko, was visiting us just now and she said that you should send them boat tickets but she wonders whether Lotte can go, and she even said Lotte will write you herself and I gave her the address — yet again. For today I kiss you, my darlings, and I thank you dear Moshko for your wonderful letter; that you want to do everything you can to take care of us and help us reassures me. God will help. Many, many kisses. I'm well and happy.

YOUR LOVING MOTHER

MY DEAR LITTLE ONES,

I'm so happy that you learn so well, and that you draw. But you're forgetting Czech! So how will we understand each other? And you, my little Tomichek, must not wet your pants because the other children will make fun of you. I'm also happy that Raya liked her Purim costume.

MANY KISSES — WRITE!

[Note in margin] About three weeks ago Weinman died. Recently, he had asked about you. I went to pay a call but she [the widow?] wasn't home.

✉

> It is not known who Weinman was, other than an acquaintance of the Froehlichs. (See P.S. to *Letter 3*.)

✉

[P.S. from Mrs Fleischmann]
DEAR IRMA,

    I am visiting with your mother and I take this opportunity to write you a few lines. Yesterday I received a letter from our Frantichek to which Ella also added a few lines. It made me very happy. I know only that they are all, thank God, well. I can't even express how much I miss them and how worried I am about my children and my darling Eva. I hope that you have good news from them and that you send them my love. Greetings to you and your dear husband and the children.

CORDIALLY,
ELLA FL.

Letter 68
From Aunt Rosa   Vienna
To Irma and Max   [No date]

DEAR EVERYBODY:

    We are leaving soon from Vienna and will see you soon.
Your mother and Erwin are well and would like to be coming,
too. Be well, see you soon.

AUNT ROSA

Letter 69
From Paula

Nurembergstrasse 32
Prague
June 11, 1941

MY DEAR PRECIOUS CHILDREN,

Friday June 6, in the morning, I couldn't even wait for the mailman because I was so sure there would be a letter from you. During the night I had so many dreams about you. I dreamed we were all together – if only it were true – but in good health and calm. Dear Erwin asked me in the morning why I was so restless in the night and why I was crying with joy until I awoke. I hugged and kissed you all so, and I couldn't let go of you. In the evening, while I was falling asleep, I was thinking of you so much – if only, dear Shishinko, I had you here again – I miss you so much, and have you only in my dreams. In my heart I have only one desire: that God, who is omnipotent, will make everything come out well and let us all be together; happy and healthy as we once were.

I loved the picture of dear Tomichek – I have it here close to me and I always look at it, it is so adorable with the playful eyes, and he looks so big, and how nicely he sits on that pony. I show it to everyone and brag. How dear father [Leopold] would have loved to see it – but not the other things. Only the good things. The other sad things he is spared. Every week I pray for him and for your father, Moshko – if only God hears me. Did you get the picture of dear father in the Stromofka? If you got it, Erwin and I will go and take more pictures and send them. Send us also more photos of you and the dear girls. His Mommy has so much pleasure from Tommy.

Ettel and Lotte complain to me. They say that you should have taken them along with you but I tell them that you couldn't even take Helgichka and Rayushka! Dear Rosa and Erna are now in Lisbon. They were in Berlin for a week. They told me they would write you. When you see Aunt Julia and sons, say hello to them and say I wish I could meet them. So now, Shishinko, maybe you have a little peace when the "little devils" are in school. You have plenty of work with my little girls. Where are the times when I could be with you and see you and help you? Where are the times when I could see you whenever I wanted? It seems so long ago, in a dream. I get such pleasure reading your news, but I would also like to hear, Moshko, that you have a job and that it pays well and is nearer to you. But I hope God has been good to you. Don't be mad at me, but it's my nature to worry about how things are and how they will turn out — here and over there. You will hear everything from Teta Rosa. If only you can write — and write soon.

Be well and happy and know your Mother loves you.

✉

Since Irma's father, Leopold, had died in 1936, Paula's reference to taking "more pictures" makes no sense in the context and must be a code. Also the Stromofka is a public park in Prague and would have been off-limits to Paula and Erwin by this time.

In June, 1941 Germany invaded Russia.

[June 11, 1941]

My dear precious children,

You'll never know how much I love your letters and how often I read them — but please don't forget your Czech! What if when I come we don't understand each other, what would I do? How happy I am that you are learning so fast and well. Whoever asks about you hears it from me! What a shame I couldn't be with you on your birthday, but I was there in spirit — and I always, always think of you. I only want to see you again and take pleasure from seeing you. And your uncle will tell you stories and play ball with you. And I? So — more kisses from your Grandmother.

If only we were with you. Then you would show us everything and we would buy clothes and hats — no?

GRANDMA

Letter 70
From Paula

Nurembergstrasse 32
Prague
June 12, 1941

[DEAR CHILDREN,]

Yesterday I was in Vinohrad and I stopped at Fleischmann's. She asked what you write — and she knows Mrs Vohraskova. She is living in one little room of her old apartment so that she can live alone. I had intended to give Teta Rosa your address but we got to talking [and I forgot]. She will get it from Edith. Now the weather is very bad, very cold. [Code?] Write soon. If only now the affidavits and boat tickets would come and would help us. Only if they are current will they be good. Tell me how Aunt Julie is. I am glad she has such good sons, but Erwin is also very good. My children, as you well know, are so good — and that gives me strength. Did you write Edith? I wonder if she will write you and if you will see each other. I wonder if they will write while they are en route — they really brag about Edith and Arnold.

This was quite a week — Uncle Adolph and Aunt Herma — she is deaf and he can't walk. Rabl cannot adjust to his wooden leg and also walks with a cane. I wanted to visit Slonitz but I couldn't work it out. I have so much to do, I am so tired in the afternoon that I must rest. And then it's evening. Time just flies by and the months are gone. I don't know Mrs Vohraskova, so it's impossible for me to get a message to her, but I would be happy if Mrs Fleischmann got news from Franta. They always ask why you don't write them. I don't believe that my little girls can't speak Czech any more since they can still write it. Shame on you, Moshko, you want them to lose it! You must speak Czech with them, and thank you for staying home with the children so Shishinko could go to the movies—was it good? So next time, go together—but what about the children? But look out, when we are with you I will babysit, though sometimes I will go to the movies too. Thank you, Shishinko, for making the children answer you in Czech, so they can speak to your mother. I am not about to learn another language, no?

MAMA

Quite possibly, Mrs Vohraskova was a relation of someone Max or Irma met in the U.S.

The reference to Aunt Julie and her "good sons" is probably a muffled protest: Fred and Richard were delaying action on an affidavit for Paula because their mother was in poor health.

Service for Jews in barber shops was limited to the hours between eight and ten a.m. [June, 1941.]

Letter 71
From Erwin

Nurembergstrasse 32
Prague
June 15, 1941

DEAR IRMA AND MOSHKO:

Nothing new to write you about us — we do the same things all the time. Medicine I do only in theory, and practice without being paid. I'm studying psychotherapy, and I'm very busy with and interested in the Rohrschach Test — I amuse myself with it. Is it widely used over there? By neurologists as well as psychologists, etc.? A New York psychiatric institute publishes a journal by Klopke, who is supposed to be a former student of Rohrschach. Dr Emil Oberholzen from Switzerland has been in the U.S. for some time, so it [the Rohrschach test] must be widely known.

So that Mother could have a little rest from cooking, she agreed to go next month for lunch to Mrs Masarkova, whom you know from Zelizy.

HEARTFELT GREETINGS,
ERWIN

You, my dear ones, know how to draw so well! Like your Mommy — or your Daddy?

Letter 72
From Paula

Nurembergstrasse 32
Prague
July 25, 1941

MY DEAR SWEET, PRECIOUS, LOVELY CHILDREN,

I longed for and waited for a letter, and now I have it. And only when I know that you are, pray God, healthy, that is everything to me. Yes, yes — it is two years and two months since we saw each other, but it is some comfort to me when I have news of you — but I am very lonesome for you. I live only to see you again and to be, with God's help, together again. And so, my sweet dear Shishinko, I could help you establish yourself and help you with everything. I always think of how much work you have, but I know dear Moshko helps you and takes care of everything. I am now, thank God, okay and dear Erwin tries to spare me a lot. It's good that I had the operation because otherwise I couldn't be doing my work now which is very important. But how my nephew behaved does not surprise us, he is incorrigible. But we trust in God, He will not forsake us. As I always say, the bigger the misery, the more God helps. I have always seen this to be true. It is important that you, dear children, work hard on our behalf — no? We have had a letter from Teta Rosa from the boat. I told her to write you right away and I gave her your address. I don't know if you [she?] can read my writing. Yesterday Kathe [Wolff] was here. She looks very bad. She promised to come back soon. They loved your letter, and said you are the only one who wishes to help me and knows my situation. I don't cook anymore, I'm too nervous in the kitchen. Four of us share the kitchen. So Erwin arranged it so that I can relax and it really does me good. But the others are very arrogant and aloof. You went so far away, Shishinko, and for such a long time. Teta Rosa sent us a half-kilogram of coffee from Lisbon but it is chicory. I think somebody switched it! Masarkova (from Zelizy) is cooking lunch and we are going over there.

MAMA

✉

The "incorrigible" nephew is probably Arnold Vogl. How he "behaved" is not known.

✉

Letter 73 Nurembergstrasse 32
From Paula   Prague
September 13, 1941

MY DEAREST, GOLDEN EVERYBODY!

We greatly enjoyed your letter and your pictures. I had them enlarged so that I can see you better. I would have liked to take you out of them and squeeze you to my heart. My dear darlings, you all look very well and the children grew so much! For the High Holidays I wish you the best that I can think of and the most heartfelt wishes for Tomichek's birthday and for you, sweet dearest Shishinko! May God keep you all well and happy, and may the Almighty grant all of our wishes. I have here a letter that has been lying around for four weeks now because we have been waiting for Erwin to add to it. He always wants to write and that's why it's still here. This week Ana Brok married Karl Mandelik. Karl comes from Solnitz — he worked in a leather tannery. Susi Schwarz married an earl, but I think he's a fake and he took her money. I wrote you about your mother, Moshko. She says she wrote you and the letters may have crossed. We are all well, thank God. Now, once more, best wishes and many kisses.

MAMA

MY DEAR LITTLE ONES:

I am very happy with your pictures — at least I can see you on a photo. Stay very, very well. Tomichek, for your birthday and for the holidays I greet you warmly.

YOUR BABICHKA

P.S. The Groviers live next to us, and they send regards. Everybody who knows you asks about you. Ludwig Freund died. Be good and well, all of you.

Dear Moshko, Irma and Little Ones!

For the holidays and for your birthday, Imsha, best wishes! We greatly enjoyed your letter and the two pictures. We are well and getting along — particularly since Mama doesn't have to do all the cooking herself. And your mother, dear Moshko, is well and is with us more often nowadays.

Erwin

Ludwig Freund was a relative on the Froehlich side. There is a strange discrepancy between Paula's statement here and Franta Porges' comment on Ludwig Freund in the Epilogue. According to Franta, Ludwig was rounded up by the Nazis as part of the reprisal for the murder of Reinhold Heydrich and subsequently murdered in Buchenwald. In June, 1941, Heydrich had replaced Von Neurath as Protector of Moravia and Bohemia. However, Paula's letter was written in September 1941 and Heydrich was not assassinated until May of 1942.

Letter 74
From Irma
To Eleanor Roosevelt   [Fall, 1941]

DEAR LADY:

The pictures of you and your family in the newspapers gave me the idea and the courage to do the unusual thing and approach you – although a stranger. I always liked and enjoyed the nice and happy expression of your face and always felt strongly attracted. I am sure you get many letters asking you for some favor. Therefore, I shall be brief.

<u>Who am I?</u> A refugee from Prague, Czechoslovakia, here with my husband and 3 children, two girls, seven and nine, and a boy two and a half years old.

<u>What do I want?</u> An affidavit for my mother and brother. We are earning enough to take care of them, but not so much that our affidavits alone would be sufficient. It is my anxious desire to give them quick and effective help that makes me turn to you. I am sure an affidavit from you as an outstanding personality would be one hundred per cent effective if only you would be willing to help me.

<u>Who is my brother?</u> Erwin Froehlich, Prague physician, 38 years old, single, lives with my mother. He is a specialist for gastroenterology and had made himself known already as an excellent young doctor by his medical ability, his good character and a number of works published in medical journals. Since the Occupation more than a year ago, he is no longer allowed to work in his profession. He and our mother were forced to move three times during one year and to share their four-room apartment with two other

families. He is now working in a social institution without pay. Some of his publications are known in this country and I feel sure that some of the specialists in the USA would be glad to give references for him if required, including Professor Dr Schindler at the University of Chicago, the inventor of the gastroscope.

Since I have no right to take much of your time with a long story, I will let these lines be enough, hoping that you will understand that behind the few facts and words given to you lies a world of anxiety and hope.

My husband and I can give you every possible assurance that my people would never be in any sense a burden to anybody should your kind help make my dreams come true and decide to sign the papers for them. They will of course live with us in our six-room apartment at the above address.

Should you decide to kindly help my dreams come true I would take the liberty of sending you the necessary forms for signature.

Very respectfully yours,

ADDRESS OFFICIAL COMMUNICATIONS TO
THE SECRETARY OF STATE
WASHINGTON, D. C.

DEPARTMENT OF STATE
WASHINGTON

In reply refer to
VD 811.111 Frohlich, Erwin

November 18, 1941

My dear Mrs. Czerner:

Your letter of October 31, 1941 addressed to
Mrs. Roosevelt, concerning the immigration visa cases
of your mother and brother and your husband's mother
has been referred to the Department of State for reply.

I am sorry to have to inform you that, since there
are no American consular offices operating in German-
occupied territories, no action may be taken on the
cases of your relatives who are residing in Prague.

The question of the issuance of Cuban visas is
one for the consideration of the appropriate officials
of that country, and should be taken up with them.

With regard to your inability to finance your
relatives' transportation to Cuba, I must say that
unfortunately the Department has no funds to be used
for this purpose.

In the event your relatives proceed to a country
where they may apply for visas, and the Department is
furnished with definite evidence concerning their departure from their present place of residence or their
actual arrival in a country where American consular
visa services are available, the necessary forms to
be completed in their behalf will be forwarded to you.

Sincerely yours,

For the Secretary of State:

G. T. Warren
A. M. Warren
Chief, Visa Division

FOR DEFENSE
BUY
UNITED
STATES
SAVINGS
BONDS
AND STAMPS

Mrs. Max Czerner,
5335 Kimbark Avenue,
Chicago, Illinois.

Letter 76 [Postcard]
From Paula
To her sister, Malva Schnurmacher   July 1, 1942

MY DEARS,

I am writing to tell you that on Monday I ~~travel~~
report. Be well — I don't know what will be with dear Erwin,
I must go alone. He wants to come with me. So — good-
bye — until we meet again —

YOURS,
PAULA

EPILOGUE

Letter 77
From Franta Porges   Prague
To Irma   April 3, 1946

Dear Cousin,

At last I have a chance to write and answer your letter of December 12 last year. Enclosed I send you all the documents which Erwin gave me for safekeeping. For me, naturally, these papers do not have as much value as they certainly will for you.

At the end, Aunt Paula lived together with Erwin in Parizska Street in Prague. There they lived in one small room. In the apartment they lived with other Jewish families (I think about four families). They shared one kitchen. My dear aunt was very unhappy because their cohabitants were hard to get along with; there were often disagreements, mainly with respect to cooking in a shared kitchen. What was that compared with what they later had to endure in Terezin!

Aunt Paula was deported a half-year before dear Erwin. Erwin wanted very much to go with his dear mother, although as a physician he did not yet have to. He stayed only after long arguments with and at the wishes of dear Aunt Paula. During that time he visited us very often. He also used to go quite often to a Mrs Pohle in Smichov. Do you know her? Her husband Dr Pohle was later with me in Terezin.

Erwin was deported about half a year later. He left at that time with a transport of Jewish physicians. After the departure of Erwin, just as after that of Aunt Paula, we never heard another word. From the Brok family who left before Erwin, also not a word.

While Erwin and Paula were still in Prague, they

looked very well. The house where they lived in Parizska Street (formerly Mikulaska and Nikolander Street) burned out completely. This street probably suffered most during the street-fighting in Prague. Just about every second house is destroyed.

Of our entire family who did not leave in time, there remains only a tiny remnant. Unaccounted for, and most probably dead, are: our dear parents; the family Schnurmacher, except for their children Aninka (who married a Gentile) and Karl who, thank God, returned after terrible suffering in concentration camps; the family Brok (five members); Uncle Edmund Freund from Domazlice; his son Ludwig, who was dragged out during the Heydrich reprisals and sent to Buchenwald where, after two weeks, he was murdered; Aunt Clara Hirschl from Steiermark; and, unfortunately, also Aunt Paula and dear Erwin; the Schanzer family and their son Otto (Hedy emigrated to England).

My brother Paul left at the last minute for England and is at present in Austria with UNRRA [United Nations Relief and Rehabilitation Administration]. He comes to see us every three to four months. He will probably marry now and leave for America after his work with UNRRA is done.

We live in our parents' house and thank God are getting along all right. If you could send us some canned meat, cigarettes, clothing, underwear, we would appreciate it. If this is too difficult, never mind.

I hope you are well and send you warmest greetings.

Yours,
Franta Porges

As this book was going to press, responses to queries made in Israel by Raya Czerner Schapiro's son, Andrew, revealed the following information:

Max's mother Bathsheva and his sister Ettel were deported to Theresienstadt in June, 1942. Bathsheva was sent to Treblinka on October 15, 1942. Ettel was gassed in Minsk in July, 1942.

The fate of Lotte Czerner remains unknown.

APPENDIX

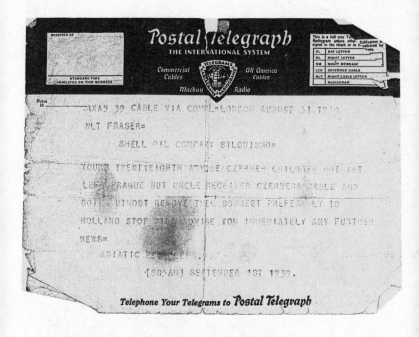

POSTAL TELEGRAM
RXa5 39 CABLE VIA COMML=LONDON AUGUST 31 1939
NLT FRASER=

      SHELL OIL COMPANY ST LOUIS MO=
YOURS TWENTY EIGHT ADVISE CZERNER CHILDREN NOT YET
LEFT PRAGUE BUT UNCLE RECEIVED CZERNERS CABLE
AND DOING UTMOST REMOVE THEM SOONEST PREFERABLY
TO HOLLAND STOP WILL ADVISE YOU IMMEDIATELY ANY FURTHER
NEWS=

      ASIATIC PETROLEUM.
          (805 AM) SEPTEMBER 1ST 1939.

C u r r i c u l u m   v i t a e.

Dr. Erwin F r o e h l i c h, born 18th March 1903 at Prague, son of Mr. Leopold Fröhligh, a merchant in Prague and of his wife, Mrs. Paula Fröhlich, whose maiden name was Porges.
After having passed the Czech Common School, he entered into the German States Middle School at Prague where he terminated his studies in 1921, being classified as "perfect". After an additional examination at the Lyceum at Prague in 1922, he started his studies at the Medical Section of the German University at Prague. The 13th January 1925 up to May 1928 he was acting as medical apprentice /"Fiscus"/ at the Internal and Neurological Section of the First Medical Clinic at Prague / Prof. Dr. R. Schmidt/ and at the psychiatrical Clinic / Prof. Dr. Otto Pötzl / of the German University.
After having been promoted Doctor of the universal medical science, the 25th May 1928 he was employed Doctor for the medical service at the Ist Medical Clinic at Prague /Prof. Dr. Rudolf Schmidt/, where he remained for almost 7 years, i.e. 31st December 1935, having managed during all this time the whole clinical ambulance for internal diseases; besides, in 1932, he was entrusted with the management of the section for stomach and intestine diseases and appointed Assistant of the Clinical Section.
Furthermore, during the absence of the Head Doctor, Mr. Wodak, Dr. Fröhlich was managing the Sanatorium for internal and nerves patients at Gräfenberg /Silesia/, where he chiefly was engaged with Psychotherapy and Diatetik. Finally, shortly before practising on his own, he was engaged at the following Vienna Institutes:
Holzknecht'sches Röntgen-Zentral-Institut. /Ass. Dr. Presser/.
Section for Stomach and Intestine Diseases /Prof. Dr. W. Zweig /.
II. Medical Section of the Child Spital / Prof. Dr. O. Porges /.
Section for Digestion Diseases / Prof. Dr. v. Noorden /.
In January 1936 he was engaged from the gastroscopis section /Ass. Dr. R. Halmos/ of the Internal Clinic /Prof. Netoušek/ at Bratislava /Slovakia/.

On account of his great experience in two special sections /internal memedicine and gastroenterology/ and after the expertise of the Chamber of Physicians as well as the Medical Board, he was appointed Specialist for Internal, Stomach, Intestine and Digestion Diseases by the Country Council of Prague, the 26th February 1936. The 15th January 1936, Dr. Fröhlich began practising on his own as a Specialist at Prague II., Washingtonova 23, and since 1938 at Prague I., Příkopy 35.
From the 1st October 1927 up to 15th February 1932, Dr. Fröhlich was registered Scholar of the Philosophic Section of the German University at Prague, where he was mainly studying philosophy and psychology.
In various Medical papers he has published 13 scientifical articles on digestion diseases.
Besides his knowledge of all usual methods for diagnostic and treatment of internal diseases – as per enclosed translations and copy of his certificate – he begs to draw the attention to his great experience in rectoscopy and proctology and especially to his experience in gastroscopy which appears to be the most efficient method of stomach examination which involves the most reliable system of recognising Gastritis, Ulcus and Cancer of stomach. Up to the present, Dr. Froehlich was executing more than 600 examinations by means of the riskless flexible gastroscop /Schindler-Wolf/. It may also be referred to his article, " Gastroskopische Befunde ..",Med.Klin.Prag-Wien-Berlin 1937,Nr.28.

ERWIN'S CURRICULUM VITAE

ENDICOTT 2-3754

EMIL A. GUTHEIL, M. D.
16 WEST 77TH STREET
(COR. CENTRAL PARK WEST)
NEW YORK, N. Y.

August 15, 1939.

TO WHOM IT MAY CONCERN:

This is to certify that Dr. Erwin Fröhlich
of Prague has worked with the undersigned at the
"Psychoanalytisches Privat-Ambulatorium" in Vienna
where he also attended courses and seminars on
psychoanalysis and psychotherapy. Dr. Fröhlich can
be warmly recommended as a conscientious and trust-
worthy man and a good psychotherapist.

Very truly yours,

N. E. A. Gutheil

Dr. E. A. Gutheil

BURRILL B. CROHN, M. D.
1075 PARK AVENUE
NEW YORK

Feb 6, 1939.

M. U. Dr. Erwin Frohlich,
35, Prikopy,
Prague, Czechoslovakia.

Dear Dr. Frohlich,

I am inclined to believe that a good gastroscopist
in this country could find himself a position with a hospital.
Just where, now, I do not know, as many of the German doctors have
brought with them their Schindler gastroscopes and everybody is
learing how to use the instrument with success.

By the time you arrive here the subject will have
become very familiar to the American public. The filed is a good
one but I do not know how to obtain an introduction to a hospital.

If you wish, I will send you a personal letter -
saying that you would be valuable and important in this country, which
letter you can turn over to your Consul.

I should be glad to do that for you.

Sincerely,

Burril Crohn

BURRILL B. CROHN, M. D.
1075 PARK AVENUE
NEW YORK

March 16, 1939.

American Consul,
2, Panska,
Prague, Bohemia.

Dear Sir,

Dr. Erwin Frohlich, living at Prague I., 35 Prikopy, CSR.,
has before you an affidavit made out by Mrs. Siegfried (Anna)
Schanzer, 565 West End Ave., New York City.

Dr. Frohlich is well known as a gastro-enterologist even
in this country. He is particularly experienced with the gastroscope. Good gastroscopists in the United States are few and far
between, due to the fact that the instrument was invented in Germany
in only the last few years and has found its greatest use and experience in the hands of Continental physicians.

We have an urgent need and use for such experienced
gastroscopists.

As a member of the Central Resettlement Committee,
representing this specialty, I can speak with some knowledge of the
situation.

I have no hesitancy is saying that Dr. Frohlich will find
immediate opportunity for work and self support.

118

Respectfully,

Burrill B. Crohn, MD.

She Remembers "Eleanor"

By Gladys Damon
Special to the Advocate

This is the centennial year of the birth of Mrs. Franklin Delano Roosevelt, affectionately remembered as "Eleanor," by the people who knew and loved her. One of those who can recall Eleanor's many humanitarian acts is Edith Vogl, 80. When efforts to save the Jews from the Holocaust often fell on the deaf ears of those in a position to help, Mrs. Vogl's life and those of her family were saved by Eleanor Roosevelt.

"I was just lucky," Mrs. Vogl told *The Advocate* recently in her Brookline home, during a wintry afternoon. "I came here just before everything happened in Czechoslovakia. We used to go skiing in Switzerland and Austria. But we couldn't go after the *Anschluss* (the annexation of Austria by Hitler's Germany in 1938). The last time we went skiing, the Nazis took us off the train at the border. It was a frightful experience. I decided then that I didn't want to live under the Nazi regime. I wanted to prepare for the future, in case anything happened.

Born in Neuri, in the Sudetenland, the Czech Bohemian Forest near Germany's Bavarian border, Edith Vogl, a musicologist, was living in Prague in 1938, where she was secretary of the Czech Philharmonic Orchestra. By a fortunate series of events, she came to Vassar College in Poughkeepsie, N.Y. in August 1938, as a member of a delegation of Czech students, to attend an international conference of the World Youth Congress. There, she met Eleanor Roosevelt, who commuted to the conference daily from her nearby home in Hyde Park, N.Y.

Most of the student group returned to Czechoslovakia and Germany. Although only three of the group were Jewish, they all ended up in concentration camps.

"I couldn't go back," she said, "and I told Mrs. Roosevelt. She told me not to worry. Mrs. Roosevelt helped me obtain my immigration visa, so I could remain here."

Immigration visas were available only to those who could meet the following requirements: if you were a member of the clergy; married to an American citizen; or had taught in your home country. Mrs. Roosevelt was instrumental in obtaining a teaching job for Vogl, at a small college in upstate New York. While she taught languages, art history and music at Keuka College for three years, Mrs. Roosevelt personally paid Edith's salary of $500 per year.

Edith's brother Arnold, who was living in Hamburg, was able to obtain a business visa to attend the World's Fair. Mrs. Roosevelt, whom Edith visited at Hyde Park, called Secretary of State Sumner Welles, who was able to obtain exit visas for their mother and sister. Since the U.S. Consulate in Prague had been closed, they had to go to Vienna to claim them.

The family was reunited in July 1941 in New York. Edith found a job and a new profession for her brother, managing a sardine factory in Eastport, Maine, a short trip by ferry from Campobello Island, New Brunswick, where the Roosevelt family had long maintained a summer home. In the meantime, Mrs. Roosevelt had established the Student Leadership Institute at Campobello, where the Vogls often visited her. And Mrs. Roosevelt visited Arnold's sardine factory, which she described in one of her daily newspaper columns, "My Day," contributing her royalties to the Vogl family.

Photo by Micki Keno

Edith Vogl

Mrs. Roosevelt also saved other Jews, contributing all the money she earned from her newspaper column, "My Day," toward their welfare, Mrs. Vogl said.

What was Eleanor Roosevelt like? "She was very generous. I learned one particular sentence from her," Mrs. Vogl said. "'Generosity is success. If you're generous with people, somehow it all comes back to you.' She lived up to this motto. How right she was! She was quite shy. She loved young people. She would much rather be with them than with 'grownups'. She wasn't vain. Her humanitarian concerns were of paramount importance to her."

During the ensuing years, the two women continued their friendship. When Edith came to Boston in 1942 to attend a seminar at Harvard, she was invited to teach at the N.E. Conservatory of Music, and later at B.U. School of Music, where she taught musicology for 13 years. Eleanor often came to Boston, where she had launched a new career at the age of 75, assuming a lectureship at Brandeis University.

"The last time I saw her was just before her death in 1962. Her estate on Campobello Island had formerly been a private enclave of exclusive summer homes for the families of the privileged. But because of her deep concern for democratic values, Eleanor wanted it to be enjoyed by the public. She had entertained many of her friends there, including many of her close, personal friends who were Jewish, such as the Henry Morgenthaus and Justice Felix Frankfurter. It has since become an international park for the public."

Mrs. Vogl also recalled attending a rally at the Hotel Bradford in Boston in 1944. Those who had been spared Hitler's madness were anxious to tell the world of the less fortunate.

Rabbis Stephen Wise and Joshua Loth Liebman addressed the audience, in an effort to draw attention to the plight of the Jews in Europe. "But there was no communication. Nobody responded," she said.

Today, Edith Vogl lives with her husband, Rudolph Garrett, whom she married in 1957, and her sister Erna, 87. Each year they share memories with friends at their New Year's Day open-house musicale. Their home is furnished with the family treasures her brother Arnold was able to salvage during his last trip from Prague in 1939.

The Jewish Advocate (Brookline, Ma.), Thursday, February 21, 1985

She Remembers "Eleanor"
By Gladys Damon (Special to *The Advocate)*

This is the centennial year of the birth of Mrs. Franklin Delano Roosevelt, affectionately remembered as "Eleanor," by the people who knew and loved her. One of those who can recall Eleanor's many humanitarian acts is Edith Vogl, 80. When efforts to save the Jews from the Holocaust often fell on the deaf ears of those in a position to help, Mrs Vogl's life and those of her family were saved by Eleanor Roosevelt.

"I was just lucky," Mrs Vogl told *The Advocate* recently in her Brookline home, during a wintry afternoon. "I came here just before everything happened in Czechoslovakia. We used to go skiing in Switzerland and Austria. But we couldn't go after the *Anschluss* (the annexation of Austria by Hitler's Germany in 1938.) The last time we went skiing, the Nazis took us off the train at the border. It was a frightful experience. I decided then that I didn't want to live under the Nazi regime. I wanted to prepare for the future, in case anything happened.

Born in Neuern, in the Sudetenland, the Czech Bohemian Forest near Germany's Bavarian border, Edith Vogl, a musicologist, was living in Prague in 1938, where she was secretary of the Czech Philharmonic Orchestra. By a fortunate series of events, she came to Vassar College in Poughkeepsie, N.Y. in August 1938, as a member of a delegation of Czech students, to attend an international conference of the World Youth Congress. There, she met Eleanor Roosevelt, who commuted to the conference daily from her near-by home in Hyde Park, N.Y.

Most of the student group returned to Czechoslovakia and Germany. Although only three of the group were Jewish, they all ended up in concentration camps.

"I couldn't go back," she said, "and I told Mrs Roosevelt. She told me not to worry. Mrs Roosevelt helped me obtain my immigration visa, so I could remain here."

Immigration visas were available only to those who could meet the following requirements: if you were a member of the clergy; married to an American citizen; or had taught in your home country. Mrs Roosevelt was instrumental in obtaining a teaching job for Vogl, at a small college in upstate New York. While she taught languages, art history and music at Keuka College for three years, Mrs Roosevelt personally paid Edith's salary of $500 per year.

Edith's brother Arnold, who was living in Hamburg, was able to obtain a business visa to attend the World's Fair. Mrs Roosevelt, whom Edith visited at Hyde Park, called Secretary of State Sumner Welles, who was able to obtain exit visas for their mother and sister. Since the U.S. Consulate in Prague had been closed, they had to go to Vienna to claim them.

The family was reunited in July 1941 in New York. Edith found a job and a new profession for her brother, managing a sardine factory in Eastport, Maine, a short trip by ferry from Campobello Island, New Brunswick, where the Roosevelt family had long maintained a summer home. In the meantime, Mrs Roosevelt had established the Student Leadership Institute at Campobello, where the Vogls often visited her. And Mrs Roosevelt visited Arnold's sardine factory, which she described in one of her daily newspaper columns, "My Day," contributing her royalties to the Vogl family.

Mrs Roosevelt also saved other Jews, contributing all the money she earned from her newspaper column, "My Day," toward their welfare, Mrs Vogl said . . . .

During the ensuing years, the two women continued their friendship. When Edith came to Boston in 1942 to attend a seminar at Harvard, she was invited to teach at the N.E. Conservatory of Music, and later at B.U. School of Music, where she taught musicology for 13 years. Eleanor often came to Boston, where she had launched a new career at the age of 75, assuming a lectureship at Brandeis University.

"The last time I saw her was just before her death in 1962. Her estate on Campobello Island had formerly been a private enclave of exclusive summer homes for the families of the privileged. But because of her deep concern for democratic values, Eleanor wanted it to be enjoyed by the public. She had entertained many of her friends there, including many of her close, personal friends who were Jewish, such as the Henry Morgenthaus and Justice Felix Frankfurter. It has since become an international park for the public."

Mrs Vogl also recalled attending a rally at the Hotel Bradford in Boston in 1944. Those who had been spared Hitler's madness were anxious to tell the world of the less fortunate. Rabbis Stephen Wise and Joshua Loth Liebman addressed the audience, in an effort to draw attention to the plight of the Jews in Europe. "But there was no communication. Nobody responded," she said.

Today, Edith Vogl lives with her husband, Rudolph Garrett, whom she married in 1957, and her sister Erna, 87. Each year they share memories with friends at their New Year's Day open-house musicale. Their home is furnished with the family treasures her brother Arnold was able to salvage during his last trip from Prague in 1939.

Excerpted from *The Jewish Advocate*, [Boston, Mass.] All rights reserved. Reprinted with permission.

YAD VASHEM יד ושם

The Holocaust Martyrs' and Heroes' Remembrance Authority רשות הזכרון לשואה ולגבורה

Mrs. Joseph Schapiro
1135 Braeburn Road
Flossmoor, IL 60422
U.S.A.

December 19th, 1988

Dear Mrs. Schapiro,

Thank you for your letter of November 2nd and for your contribution (receipt enclosed).

We were able to trace the fate of your relatives in our records and can give you following information:

1. Paula Froehlichova b. 23.10.76,
   Was deported from Prague to Theresienstadt on 9.7.1942, transport No. AAp 860. From Theresienstadt she was deported to Treblinka on 19.10. 1942, transport No. Bw 796.

2. Mr. Erwin Froehlich b. 18.3.03,
   Was deported from Prague to Theresiensatadt on 20.11.1942, tranport No. Cc 266. From Theresienstadt he was deported to Auschwitz on 21.1.1943, transport No. Cq 539.

enc. copies from the original transport lists.

Sincerely yours,

Esth Aran

Esther Aran

Archives

ת.ד. 3477, ירושלים 91034, טל. 531202, טלקס: YADVA 26573 P.O.B. 3477, JERUSALEM 91043, TEL. 531202, TELEX 26573 YADVA

TRANSPORT LIST, PRAGUE TO THERESIENSTADT, DATED JULY 9, 1942.

This is a copy of the list of deportees to the camp at Theresienstadt (Terezin) with their occupations, birth-dates and Prague address. Paula Froehlich appears as No. 860. The "Bw 796," scribbled in later, indicates the transport code and individual number of Paula's final journey from Terezin.

Osten 19.X 1942

064/309

781	Friedländer Emma	ohne	29.12.67	614/AAw
782	Dlouhý Emilie	ohne	22.12.68	750/AAw ✓
783	Fischer Emilie	Haushalt	8.2.67	836/AAp ✓
784	Pokorný Pauline	ohne	30.4.66	952/AAw ✓
785	Weinberger Rosa	Haushalt	29.6.64	956/AAw ✓
786	Propper Klara	Haushalt	3.7.72	959/AAw ✓
787	Fischer Erna	Haushalt	22.12.76	837/AAp ✓
788	Löwy Gustav	ohne	11.2.68	970/AAw ✓
789	Hirsch Dr.Julius	Arbeiter	14.9.67	975/AAw ✓
790	Fröhlich Alois	ohne	16.9.69	856/AAp ✓
791	Fröhlich Josefa	Haushalt	6.6.68	857/AAp ✓
792	Nathan Aloisie	ohne	1.3.76	985/AAw ✓
793	Fröhlich Alfred	ohne	31.3.72	855/AAp ✓
794	König Ida	Haushalt	24.2.76	485/Bg ✓
795	Riegl Marie	Haushalt	29.12.71	636/Bg ✓
796	Fröhlich Paula	Haushalt	23.10.76	860/AAp ✓
797	Stamm Valerie S.	Haushalt	6.9.69	787-IV/10 ✓
798	Seeger Julius I.	Hilfsarb.	23.1.70	677-IV/2 ✓
799	Seeger Klothilde S.	Haushalt	1.2.64	678-IV/2 ✓
800	Klauber Eugenie	Haushalt	31.12.73	164/AAe ✓
801	Löwy Berta	Haushalt	6.1.73	4/At ✓
802	Deutsch Josef	ohne	19.12.68	61/At ✓
803	Löbl Irma	Haushalt	14.4.82	68/At ✓
804	Löbl Alfred	Hilfsarb.	5.10.6.	67/At ✓
805	Fröhlich Sidonie	Haushalt	3.3.69	861/AAp ✓
806	Edelstein Berta	Haushalt	26.2.72	178/At ✓
807	Ehrlich Kamila	ohne	26.3.73	175/At ✓
808	Dubsky Berta	Haushalt	23.2.74	193/At ✓
809	Dubsky Adele	ohne	24.3.74	196/At ✓
810	Elišák Hermine	Haushalt	26.6.71	229/At ✓

Bw

TRANSPORT LIST, TEREZIN TO "THE EAST", DATED OCTOBER 19, 1942

Copy of list of deportees to "the East" [Osten] from Terezin, with occupation, birthdate, transport code and number. Paula is number 796. It was learned later that transport Bw went to Treblinka.

TRANSPORT LIST, PRAGUE TO TEREZIN, DATED NOVEMBER 20, 1942
List of deportees, mainly medical doctors ("MUDr") from the Jewish Hospital (JKG), with their occupations, birthdates and Prague address. The hand-written numbers and letters refer to later transport from Terezin to the East. Erwin's name is the sixth entry and contains the notation, 539 Cq,

lfd. Nr. Name u. Vorname	Beruf	Geb. Dat.	Alte Tr. Nr.
511 Žalud Siegmund	ohne	22.7.1881	614/Bz
512 Žalud Henriette	ohne	19.12.1889	615/Bz
513 Winternitz Otto	Arbeiter	28.4.1900	621/Bz
514 Winternitz Rosa	Haushalt	2.10.1908	623/Bz
515 Winternitz Hana	Schülerin	5.7.1933	624/Bz
516 Winternitz Lilly	Schülerin	29.7.1929	627/Bz
517 Mračno Anna	Elektroarb.	24.5.1892	622/Bz
518 Kohn Alice	Modistin	14.1.1893	224/Cm
519 Kolmann Josef	Arbeiter	12.8.1924	628/Bz
520 Salus Josefine	Haushalt	29.3.1885	641/Bz
521 Kaufmann Klara	Haushalt	22.7.1913	642/Bz
522 Porges Emil	Arbeiter	6.7.1892	644/Bz
523 Porges Hilde	Haushalt	21.1.1899	645/Bz
524 Fischl Richard	Arbeiter	4.4.1917	649/Bz
525 Salus Ladislaus	Arbeiter	18.7.1912	640/Bz
526 Lustig Anna	Handelsgeh.	13.3.1916	307/Cl
527 Kuh Sofie	Haushalt	26.4.1880	308/Cl
528 Lang Elsa	Haushalt	12.3.1883	678/AAt
529 Heller Josef	Arbeiter	23.12.1890	25/Ca
530 Heller Martha	Haushakt	11.1.1903	26/Ca
531 Heller Otto	Lehrling	21.9.1924	27/Ca
532 Heller Sidonius	Schüler	6.3.1927	28/Ca
533 Steiner Viktor	Ing.Chem.	14.3.1900	478/Cl
534 Nettel Kurt	Arbeiter	4.5.1905	485/Cl
535 Nettel Olga	Haushalt	24.1.1910	486/Cl
536 Nettel Paul	Kind	13.3.1934	487/Cl
537 Kahn Friedrich	Arbeiter	30.11.1900	230/Cm
538 Schindler Bernard	Arbeiter	14.9.1921	96/Ca
539 Fröhlich Dr. Erwin	Arzt	18.3.1903	266/Ca
540 Altschul Ludmila	Haushalt	17.7.1889	259/Cl

Cqu

TRANSPORT LIST, TEREZIN TO "THE EAST," DATED JANUARY 21, 1943
List of deportees to "the East" [Osten] from Terezin, with occupation, birth-date, and transport number of arrival to Terezin. Erwin appears as No. 539. This transport went to Auschwitz [Oswiecim], according to later documentation.

LIST OF TRANSPORTS FROM THERESIENSTADT TO THE EAST

Designation	Destination		Number of Deportees	Number of Survivors
O	Riga	9.1.42	1000	102
P	Riga	15.1.42	1000	15
Aa	Izbice	11.3.42	1001	6
Ab	Izbice	17.3.42	1000	3
Ag	Piaski	1.4.42	1000	4
Ap	Rejowiece	18.4.42	1000	2
Al	Lublin	23.4.42	1000	1
An	Warsaw	25.4.42	1000	8
Aq	Izbice	27.4.42	1000	1
Ar	Zamosce	28.4.42	1000	5
As	Zamosce	30.4.42	1000	19
Ax	Sobibor (?)	9.5.42	1000	—
Ay	Lublin (?)	17.5.42	1000	—
Az	Lublin	25.5.42	1000	1
AAk	Trawniky (?)	12.6.42	1000	—
AAi	(?)	13.6.42	1000	—
AAx	Minsk	14.7.42	1000	2
AAy	(?)	28.7.42	1000	—
AAz	Maly Trostinec	4.8.42	1000	2
Bb	(?)	20.8.42	1000	—
Bc	Maly Trostinec (?)	25.8.42	1000	1
Be	Raasika	1.9.42	1000	45
Bk	Maly Trostinec	8.9.42	1000	4
Bo	Maly Trostinec (?)	19.9.42	2000	—
Bp	Maly Trostinec (?)	21.9.42	2020	—
Bn	Maly Trostinec (?)	22.9.42	1000	1
Bq	Maly Trostinec (?)	23.9.42	1980	—
Br	Maly Trostinec (?)	26.9.42	2004	—
Bs	Maly Trostinec (?)	29.9.42	2000	—
Bt	Treblinka (?)	5.10.42	1000	—
Bu	Treblinka	8.10.42	1000	2
Bv	Treblinka	15.10.42	1998	—
Bw	Treblinka	19.10.42	1984	—
Bx	Treblinka	22.10.42	2018	—
By	Osviecim	26.10.42	1866	28
Cq	Osviecim	20.1.43	2000	2
Cr	Osviecim	23.1.43	2000	3
Cs	Osviecim	26.1.43	1000	39

Designation	Destination		Number of Deportees	Number of Survivors
Ct	Osviecim	29.1.43	1000	23
Cu	Osviecim	1.2.43	1001	29
Dl	Osviecim	6.9.43	2479	26
Dm	Osviecim	6.9.43	2528	11
Dn/a	Osviecim	5.10.43	53	—
Dr	Osviecim	15.12.43	2504	262
Ds	Osviecim	18.12.43	2503	443
Dx	Bergen-Belsen	20.3.44	45	—
Dz	Osviecim	15.5.44	2503	119
Ea	Osviecim	16.5.44	2500	5
Eb	Osviecim	18.5.44	2500	261
Eh	Bergen-Belsen	1.7.44	10	—
Eg	Bergen-Belsen	4.7.44	15	—
Ej	Bergen-Belsen	27.9.44	20	—
Ek	Osviecim	28.9.44	2499	371
El	Osviecim	29.9.44	1500	76
Em	Osviecim	1.10.44	1500	293
En	Osviecim	4.10.44	1500	127
Eo	Osviecim	6.10.44	1550	76
Ep	Osviecim	9.10.44	1600	22
Eq	Osviecim	12.10.44	1500	74
Er	Osviecim	16.10.44	1500	110
Es	Osviecim	19.10.44	1500	51
Et	Osviecim	23.10.44	1715	159
Ev	Osviecim	28.10.44	2038	137
Totals			86934	2971

The Fate of the Transports to the East

"October 19, 1942: 1984 prisoners (Transport Bw).
From Theresienstadt to the East, probably to Treblinka, where other prisoners recognized their luggage by the letters and numbers of the transport. No deportee from these transports returned; it must be assumed that all prisoners perished in Treblinka."

"January 20, 1943: 2,000 prisoners(Transport Cq)
From Theresienstadt to Osviecim, where 160 young women and 80 young men were selected for work on the arrival of the transport while the remaining 1,760 prisoners were taken in lorries to the gas chambers. With the exception of two women, the surviving prisoners perished within six weeks."

NOTES

Information on Nazi laws and edicts was taken from John G. Lexa, "Anti-Jewish Laws and Regulations in the Protectorate of Bohemia and Moravia," in *The Jews of Czechoslovakia*, ed. Avigdor Dagan, Gertrude Hirschler and Lewis Weiner, III (Philadelphia: The Jewish Publication Society, 1984), 75-103.

Pages 38-41. See Ruth Bondy, *"Elder of the Jews": Jakob Edelstein of Theresienstadt*, trans. Evelyn Abel (New York: Grove Press, 1981), pp. 145-6.

Pages 212-213. See Zdenek Lederer, *Ghetto Theresienstadt* (New York: Howard Fertig, 1983), pp. 223-4; 250-1.

NAME INDEX